Python Interview Secrets: Answer Like A Pro And Get Hired In 30 Days

Author: Yash d.

ISBN-13: 9798301249884

Cover design by: Art Painter
Library of Congress Control Number: 2018675309
Printed in the United States of America

To all the aspiring Python developers,
who tirelessly strive to crack that one big interview,
and to those who believe that mastering Python
is not just about code, but the art of problem-solving.
This book is for you – a guide, a companion, and a path to
success.
May this help you turn your passion for Python
into a thriving career, one line of code at a time.

To the countless mentors and communities
who inspire, guide, and push us to reach greater heights.
Your contributions are the unseen foundation
upon which this book is built.

CONTENTS

PREFACE

In the fast-paced world of technology, Python has emerged as one of the most powerful and versatile programming languages. Its popularity has soared in industries ranging from web development and data science to artificial intelligence and automation. But, as demand for Python skills grows, so does the competition. In the race to land that coveted Python developer position, many candidates often struggle to showcase their skills effectively in interviews.

Python Interview Secrets: Answer Like a Pro and Get Hired in 30 Days is designed to bridge the gap between technical knowledge and real-world interview success. Whether you are just starting your career or looking to elevate your existing Python expertise, this book is here to equip you with the tools to ace your interview in a month's time. This isn't just another book filled with theory's a strategic guide that focuses on what really matters when you're in the hot seat: **answering like a pro**.

This book is structured to help you build a clear and concise path to Python interview success. In the next 30 days, we will break down complex interview questions and provide **straightforward, actionable answers** to give you the confidence to tackle any challenge thrown your way. Each chapter is packed with the most commonly asked Python interview questions, **real-world examples**, and **pro tips** that will help you stand out from the crowd.

Our approach is simple: **Practice makes perfect**, but knowing *how* to approach those questions is even more crucial. Whether it's fundamental topics like Python data structures or advanced concepts like decorators and concurrency, this book will arm you with the knowledge and techniques to demonstrate your proficiency. The goal isn't just to answer questions correctly; it's to present yourself as a skilled and confident Python expert who can solve problems efficiently.

But there's more to succeeding in an interview than just solving coding challenges. Beyond your technical expertise, interviews are about showcasing your **problem-solving approach, communication skills**, and your ability to remain calm under pressure. That's why this book also covers the often-overlooked areas of **interview mastery**, including resume building, handling behavioral questions, and negotiating your job offer.

With a proven approach designed to maximize your chances in Python interviews, this book will guide you through every step of the process. Whether you are a fresh graduate eager to dive into the world of Python programming or an experienced developer looking for the perfect role, you will find practical strategies and expert advice that will empower you to **answer like a pro** and get hired in just 30 days.

Let's get started, and may this book be your guide to landing your dream Python developer job!

YOUR 30-DAY PYTHON INTERVIEW BLUEPRINT

Congratulations on Taking the First Step!

Congratulations! By picking up *Python Interview Secrets: Answer Like a Pro and Get Hired in 30 Days*, you've taken an essential step toward acing your Python interview and landing your dream job. The journey from preparation to success in technical interviews can seem daunting, but with the right strategy, discipline, and guidance, it's absolutely achievable. This book is your trusted companion, guiding you through the essential topics, problem-solving techniques, and interview tactics that will help you stand out from the competition.

Why 30 Days?

Thirty days might sound like a short time to prepare, but it's also long enough to create a meaningful impact if approached strategically. This timeline isn't about cramming but about targeted learning. You'll focus on mastering the most commonly asked Python interview questions, building problem-solving skills, and honing your confidence through consistent practice.

The Roadmap to Success

Week 1: Laying the Foundations

In the first week, you'll focus on strengthening your understanding of Python fundamentals. Think of this as building the bedrock for the more advanced concepts you'll encounter later. Key areas to focus on include:

1. **Core Python Concepts**: Variables, data types, operators, and control flow structures.
2. **Data Structures**: Master lists, tuples, sets, and dictionaries.
3. **Functions**: Learn how to write reusable and efficient code with Python functions and lambdas.

The goal this week is to ensure that you can confidently discuss these topics in an interview setting. Practice writing small programs to reinforce your knowledge and get comfortable solving problems independently.

Week 2: Diving Deeper

The second week is about advancing your knowledge. Here, you'll explore object-oriented programming (OOP), file handling, and error management. These are critical areas that interviewers love to test. Focus on:

1. **OOP Principles**: Learn about classes, objects, inheritance, polymorphism, and encapsulation. Be prepared to explain these concepts with real-world examples.
2. **File Handling**: Understand reading, writing, and managing files in Python.
3. **Exception Handling**: Master try-except blocks and learn to debug code effectively.

During this week, practice solving coding problems that integrate these concepts. For example, create a program that reads data from a file, processes it using a class, and gracefully handles errors.

Week 3: Mastering Advanced Concepts

Now that your basics are strong, it's time to dive into advanced topics that often appear in interviews. These include:

1. **Decorators and Generators**: Understand their purpose and how they simplify complex tasks.
2. **Concurrency and Asynchronous Programming**: Get a basic grasp of threading, multiprocessing, and async/await.
3. **Popular Libraries**: Familiarize yourself with libraries like numpy, pandas, and matplotlib, as they often come up in data-related roles.

This week is also a great time to start solving algorithmic problems. Use platforms like LeetCode, HackerRank, or GeeksforGeeks to practice coding challenges related to searching, sorting, and recursion.

Week 4: Polishing and Mock Interviews

The final week is all about sharpening your skills and preparing for the interview experience itself. This involves:

1. **Solving Common Python Interview Questions**: Review a curated list of frequently asked questions and practice answering them succinctly.
2. **Mock Interviews**: Conduct mock interviews with peers or mentors to simulate the pressure of a real interview.
3. **Behavioral Questions**: Prepare responses to common HR questions that demonstrate your problem-solving mindset

and team spirit.

By the end of Week 4, you should feel confident in your technical knowledge, coding skills, and ability to communicate effectively in interviews.

A Daily Plan for Maximum Efficiency

To make the most of your 30 days, follow a structured daily schedule:

1. **Morning (1-2 hours)**: Review theory and concepts. Use this time to read, watch tutorials, or study from this book.
2. **Afternoon (1-2 hours)**: Solve coding problems. Practice on coding platforms to apply what you've learned.
3. **Evening (1 hour)**: Reflect on your progress, revise key concepts, and identify areas that need improvement.

Remember, consistency is key. Even if you have just an hour a day, use it wisely to make steady progress.

Tips to Maximize Your Success

1. Understand the "Why" Behind the Questions

Interviewers don't just want to know if you can code—they want to see how you think. When preparing answers, focus on explaining your thought process clearly. For example, when solving a problem, describe why you chose a particular data structure or algorithm.

2. Practice Problem Solving Daily

The best way to prepare for coding interviews is through

hands-on practice. Dedicate time every day to solving problems, starting with easier ones and gradually moving to more complex challenges.

3. Learn to Communicate Effectively

In interviews, how you communicate your solution is just as important as the solution itself. Practice explaining your code, even if you're working alone. This habit will help you articulate your thoughts better during the actual interview.

4. Stay Updated with Python Trends

Python is constantly evolving, with new libraries and features being introduced regularly. Stay informed about the latest updates, as interviewers may test your knowledge of Python's current capabilities.

5. Embrace Feedback

If you're conducting mock interviews or solving problems on coding platforms, pay attention to feedback. Understanding your mistakes and learning from them is crucial to improving your performance.

Final Words

This chapter is your starting point for an incredible journey. Remember, preparation isn't just about studying—it's about building confidence, honing problem-solving skills, and believing in yourself. The next 30 days will challenge you, but they will also transform you into a Python interview pro.

Let's dive into the next chapters and take the first steps toward your dream job. You've got this!

PYTHON BASICS DEMYSTIFIED

Below are essential Python interview questions and professional answers designed to help you confidently ace your technical interviews. This chapter focuses on fundamental topics like syntax, variables, and data types.

1. What are Python's key features?

Answer:
Python is:

- **Interpreted**: Code is executed line by line.
- **Dynamically typed**: Variable types are determined at runtime, not in advance.
- **High-level**: It abstracts low-level operations like memory management.
- **Object-oriented and functional**: It supports multiple programming paradigms.
- **Extensible**: You can integrate C/C++ libraries for performance.
- **Richly supported**: Has a vast library ecosystem for various applications.

2. How do you declare a variable in Python?

Answer:
In Python, declaring a variable is straightforward as no explicit data type declaration is needed. You can assign a value to a

variable directly:

```
x = 10  # Integer
y = 3.14  # Float
name = "Alice"  # String
```

Variables are dynamically typed, meaning their type can change during execution:

```
x = 10
x = "Now I'm a string"  # Valid in Python.
```

---

3. What are Python's built-in data types?

Answer:
Key data types include:

- **Numeric Types**: int, float, complex
- **Text Type**: str
- **Sequence Types**: list, tuple, range
- **Mapping Type**: dict
- **Set Types**: set, frozenset
- **Boolean Type**: bool
- **Binary Types**: bytes, bytearray, memoryview

For example:

```
num = 42  # int
pi = 3.14  # float
is_python_fun = True  # bool
fruits = ["apple", "banana", "cherry"]  # list
```

---

4. How does Python handle type conversion?

Answer:
Python supports both **implicit** and **explicit** type conversion:

- **Implicit**: Python automatically converts compatible types.

```
x = 10  # int
y = 3.14  # float
result = x + y  # Automatically converted to float
```

- **Explicit**: You manually convert types using functions like int(), float(), str().

```
x = "100"
y = int(x)  # Explicitly convert to integer
z = float(x)  # Convert to float
```

---

5. What is the difference between is and ==?

Answer:

== checks for value equality:

```
a = [1, 2, 3]
b = [1, 2, 3]
print(a == b)  # True (values are the same)
```

-

is checks for object identity (whether two variables point to the same object in memory):

```
print(a is b)  # False (different memory locations)
```

-

---

6. How does Python handle mutable and immutable types?

Answer:

- **Immutable Types**: Cannot be changed after creation. Examples: int, float, str, tuple.

```
x = "hello"
x[0] = "H"  # Error! Strings are immutable.
```

- **Mutable Types**: Can be modified. Examples: list, dict, set.

```
lst = [1, 2, 3]
lst[0] = 10  # Allowed, as lists are mutable.
```

---

7. Explain Python's string slicing and indexing.

Answer:
Python allows accessing parts of a string using indices:

```
s = "Python"
print(s[0])  # 'P' (first character)
print(s[-1])  # 'n' (last character)
print(s[1:4])  # 'yth' (from index 1 to 3)
```

- **Default slicing behavior**:
  - s[start:stop:step]
  - Omitting start starts at the beginning, omitting stop goes to the end.

Example:

```
print(s[:3])  # 'Pyt'
print(s[::2])  # 'Pto' (every second character)
```

---

8. What is the difference between a list and a tuple?

Answer:

Feature	List	Tuple

Mutability	Mutable	Immutable
Syntax	[]	()
Performance	Slower	Faster (immutable)
Use Cases	Dynamic data	Fixed, constant data

Examples:

```
# List
fruits = ["apple", "banana", "cherry"]
fruits[0] = "orange" # Allowed

# Tuple
coordinates = (10, 20)
coordinates[0] = 15 # Error! Tuples are immutable.
```

9. How does Python manage memory for variables?

Answer:
Python uses an **automatic memory management system** with reference counting and garbage collection:

- Objects are reference-counted; when no references remain, the memory is reclaimed.
- Cyclic garbage collector handles objects involved in reference cycles.

10. Explain the difference between None, 0, and False.

Answer:

- None: Represents the absence of a value. It's of type NoneType.
- 0: Represents a numeric value (zero). It's of type int.
- False: A Boolean value indicating a logical false.

Example:

```
x = None
y = 0
z = False

print(x == y)  # False
print(y == z)  # True (0 is considered False in Boolean context)
```

---

11. What is unpacking in Python?

Answer:
Unpacking allows assigning elements of a collection (like a list or tuple) to variables in a single operation:

```
a, b, c = [1, 2, 3]
print(a)  # 1
print(b)  # 2
print(c)  # 3
```

Unpacking with *:

```
a, *b, c = [1, 2, 3, 4, 5]
print(a)  # 1
print(b)  # [2, 3, 4]
print(c)  # 5
```

---

12. How do Python's id() and type() functions work?

Answer:
- id(obj): Returns the memory address of an object.
- type(obj): Returns the type of an object.

Example:

```
x = 42
print(id(x)) # Memory address of x
print(type(x)) # <class 'int'>
```

13. What is the output of the following code? Why?

```
a = [1, 2, 3]
b = a
b.append(4)
print(a)
```

Answer:
Output: [1, 2, 3, 4]
Explanation: Both a and b point to the same object in memory.
Changes made via b affect a.

14. Write a program to swap two variables without using a third variable.

Answer:

```
x = 5
y = 10
x, y = y, x
print(x, y) # Output: 10, 5
```

15. What is the difference between del and garbage collection?

Answer:
- del: Deletes a reference to an object, but the object may not be removed from memory if other references exist.
- **Garbage collection**: Automatically frees memory occupied by objects no longer referenced.

Example:

```
a = [1, 2, 3]
b = a
del a
print(b)  # [1, 2, 3] (object still exists as b refers to it)
```

This chapter equips you with concise and practical answers to essential Python basics, ensuring a confident start to your interview preparation.

CONTROL FLOW ESSENTIALS

Control flow structures are fundamental to programming and are frequently tested in Python interviews. Below are **interview-style questions and answers** to help you master this topic.

Question 1: What is the difference between if, elif, and else in Python?

Answer (Pro Level):

- The if statement evaluates a condition. If the condition is True, the block of code inside it is executed.
- The elif statement (short for "else if") provides additional conditions to check when the first if condition evaluates to False.
- The else statement acts as a fallback and executes when all previous conditions (if and elif) are False.

Example:

```
x = 10
if x > 15:
    print("Greater than 15")
elif x > 5:
    print("Between 6 and 15")
else:
    print("5 or less")
```

Pro Tip: Keep conditions exclusive where possible to avoid ambiguity. Use elif to handle intermediate cases and else for a default action.

Question 2: Can you use multiple conditions in a single if statement?

Answer (Pro Level):
Yes, Python allows the use of logical operators (and, or, not) to combine multiple conditions within a single if statement.

Example:

```
age = 25
income = 50000

if age > 18 and income > 30000:
    print("Eligible for credit card")
else:
    print("Not eligible")
```

Pro Insight: Logical operators evaluate from left to right. Using parentheses for clarity is recommended when combining multiple conditions.

Question 3: How does Python handle nested if statements?

Answer (Pro Level):
Nested if statements allow you to include another if inside an outer if block. This is useful when decisions depend on hierarchical conditions.

Example:

```
num = 15
if num > 10:
```

```
if num % 2 == 0:
    print("Even number greater than 10")
else:
    print("Odd number greater than 10")
else:
    print("10 or less")
```

Pro Tip: Avoid deeply nested if statements when possible. Flatten your logic using logical operators for better readability.

Question 4: Explain Python's while loop with an example.

Answer (Pro Level):
A while loop repeatedly executes a block of code as long as its condition evaluates to True. If the condition becomes False, the loop stops.

Example:

```
count = 0
while count < 5:
    print("Count:", count)
    count += 1
```

Pro Insight: Ensure that the loop condition will eventually become False. Infinite loops can occur if the condition never changes or is always True.

Question 5: What is the difference between break and continue in loops?

Answer (Pro Level):
- break: Exits the loop prematurely, regardless of the loop condition.
- continue: Skips the current iteration and jumps to the next iteration.

Example:

```
for i in range(10):
    if i == 5:
        break  # Stops the loop when i is 5
    elif i % 2 == 0:
        continue  # Skips even numbers
    print(i)
```

Pro Tip: Use break to terminate loops based on a condition, and continue to refine logic without ending the loop.

Question 6: How can you create an infinite loop in Python? Is it recommended?

Answer (Pro Level):
An infinite loop can be created using a while loop with a condition that is always True. While it can be useful for certain tasks like servers or event listeners, it must include a condition to exit safely.

Example:

```
while True:
    command = input("Enter command (type 'exit' to quit): ")
    if command == 'exit':
        break
```

Pro Tip: Always implement an exit condition (e.g., break) to avoid unintentional resource consumption.

Question 7: Explain the for loop in Python and how it is different from while.

Answer (Pro Level):

- A for loop iterates over a sequence (like a list, tuple, or

string) directly.
- A while loop relies on a condition and is typically used when the number of iterations isn't predefined.

Example:

```
names = ["Alice", "Bob", "Charlie"]
for name in names:
    print("Hello,", name)
```

Pro Insight: Use for loops for iterating over collections and while loops for conditions that require dynamic evaluation.

Question 8: How does Python's range() function work in a for loop?

Answer (Pro Level):
The range() function generates a sequence of numbers, commonly used in for loops.

Example:

```
for i in range(1, 10, 2):  # Start at 1, end before 10, increment by 2
    print(i)
```

Pro Tip: Remember that range() is exclusive of its end value and supports three arguments: start, stop, and step.

Question 9: What is a pass statement, and when would you use it?

Answer (Pro Level):
The pass statement is a placeholder that does nothing when executed. It's used when a statement is syntactically required but no action is needed.

Example:

```
for i in range(5):
    if i == 3:
        pass  # Placeholder for future code
    else:
        print(i)
```

Pro Insight: Use pass for prototyping or when you're planning to implement functionality later.

Question 10: How do Python's else blocks work with loops?

Answer (Pro Level):
Python allows else blocks to be used with for and while loops. The else block executes only if the loop completes without encountering a break.

Example:

```
for i in range(5):
    if i == 3:
        break
    print(i)
else:
    print("Loop completed successfully")
```

Pro Tip: The else clause in loops is often overlooked. It can be useful for signaling completion or additional logic.

Question 11: How can you use enumerate() in a for loop?

Answer (Pro Level):
The enumerate() function adds a counter to an iterable, returning both the index and the value.

Example:

```
fruits = ["apple", "banana", "cherry"]
for index, fruit in enumerate(fruits):
    print(f"Index {index}: {fruit}")
```

Pro Insight: Use enumerate() to keep track of the iteration index while iterating over a sequence.

Question 12: What is a zip() function in Python? How is it used in loops?

Answer (Pro Level):
The zip() function combines two or more iterables into tuples, enabling parallel iteration.

Example:

```
names = ["Alice", "Bob", "Charlie"]
scores = [85, 92, 78]
for name, score in zip(names, scores):
    print(f"{name} scored {score}")
```

Pro Insight: Use zip() for situations where multiple sequences need to be processed together.

WORKING WITH PYTHON'S DATA STRUCTURES

In this chapter, we'll dive into the most essential data structures in Python: **lists**, **tuples**, **dictionaries**, and **sets**. These are the foundational building blocks that help in solving various coding challenges, and mastering them is crucial for acing your Python interview. The following interview questions and answers will focus on practical, real-world examples where these data structures are applied.

1. Lists

Q1: How do you create a list in Python, and how do you access an element by index?

A1: A list in Python is created by enclosing elements in square brackets [], separated by commas. To access an element, use zero-based indexing.

```python
my_list = [10, 20, 30, 40, 50]
print(my_list[2]) # Output: 30
```

In this example, my_list[2] accesses the element at index 2 (which is 30).

Q2: How can you remove an item from a list in Python?

A2: You can use the remove() method or the pop() method to remove an item. The remove() method removes the first occurrence of the specified value, while pop() removes an item at a specific index.

```
my_list = [10, 20, 30, 40, 50]
my_list.remove(30) # Removes the first occurrence of 30
print(my_list) # Output: [10, 20, 40, 50]

# Using pop()
removed_item = my_list.pop(1) # Removes item at index 1
print(my_list) # Output: [10, 40, 50]
print(removed_item) # Output: 20
```

Q3: What is the difference between append() and extend() in lists?

A3: The append() method adds a single element to the end of the list, while extend() takes an iterable and adds all its elements to the list.

```
my_list = [1, 2, 3]
my_list.append(4) # Adds a single element
print(my_list) # Output: [1, 2, 3, 4]

my_list.extend([5, 6]) # Adds all elements of the iterable
print(my_list) # Output: [1, 2, 3, 4, 5, 6]
```

2. Tuples

Q4: What is the difference between a list and a tuple in Python?

A4: The main difference is that **tuples** are **immutable**, meaning once created, their elements cannot be changed. Lists are **mutable**, and their elements can be modified.

```
my_tuple = (1, 2, 3)
# my_tuple[0] = 10  # This will raise an error because tuples are
immutable
```

Q5: How do you create a tuple with a single element?

A5: To create a tuple with a single element, you must include a trailing comma.

```
single_element_tuple = (10,) # Correct
```

Without the comma, Python will treat it as a regular parenthesis.

```
not_a_tuple = (10) # This is just an integer, not a tuple
```

Q6: Can you unpack a tuple in Python?

A6: Yes, tuple unpacking allows you to assign the elements of a tuple to multiple variables.

```
my_tuple = (1, 2, 3)
a, b, c = my_tuple # Unpacking
print(a, b, c) # Output: 1 2 3
```

3. Dictionaries

Q7: How do you create a dictionary in Python, and how can you access a value by key?

A7: A dictionary in Python is created using curly braces {}, with key-value pairs separated by colons. You access a value by its key using square brackets.

```
my_dict = {"name": "Alice", "age": 30}
```

```
print(my_dict["name"]) # Output: Alice
```

Q8: How do you handle a situation where a key may not exist in the dictionary?

A8: You can use the get() method, which allows you to specify a default value if the key doesn't exist.

```
my_dict = {"name": "Alice", "age": 30}
print(my_dict.get("address", "Not Available"))   # Output: Not Available
```

Q9: How can you remove a key-value pair from a dictionary?

A9: You can use the pop() method to remove a key-value pair and get the value of the removed item.

```
my_dict = {"name": "Alice", "age": 30}
removed_value = my_dict.pop("age")
print(my_dict) # Output: {'name': 'Alice'}
print(removed_value) # Output: 30
```

Q10: How do you merge two dictionaries in Python?

A10: In Python 3.5 and above, you can use the ** unpacking operator to merge dictionaries.

```
dict1 = {"a": 1, "b": 2}
dict2 = {"c": 3, "d": 4}
merged_dict = {**dict1, **dict2}
print(merged_dict) # Output: {'a': 1, 'b': 2, 'c': 3, 'd': 4}
```

---

4. Sets

Q11: What is a set in Python, and how is it different from a list?

A11: A set is an unordered collection of unique elements. Unlike lists, sets do not allow duplicate values and do not maintain the order of elements.

```
my_set = {1, 2, 3, 4, 5}
print(my_set) # Output: {1, 2, 3, 4, 5}
my_set.add(6) # Adding an element
print(my_set) # Output: {1, 2, 3, 4, 5, 6}
```

Q12: How do you remove duplicates from a list using sets?

A12: You can convert a list into a set, which automatically removes duplicates, and then convert it back to a list if necessary.

```
my_list = [1, 2, 3, 3, 4, 5, 5]
unique_list = list(set(my_list))
print(unique_list) # Output: [1, 2, 3, 4, 5]
```

Q13: How do you perform set operations like union, intersection, and difference in Python?

A13: You can perform set operations using built-in methods:

- **Union:** Combines two sets.

```
set1 = {1, 2, 3}
set2 = {3, 4, 5}
print(set1 | set2) # Output: {1, 2, 3, 4, 5}
```

- **Intersection:** Returns common elements.

```
print(set1 & set2) # Output: {3}
```

- **Difference:** Returns elements in the first set but not in the second.

```
print(set1 - set2)  # Output: {1, 2}
```

---

5. Mixed Data Structure Operations

Q14: How can you iterate over a dictionary in Python?

A14: You can iterate over a dictionary using items(), keys(), or values() methods.

```
my_dict = {"name": "Alice", "age": 30}
for key, value in my_dict.items():
    print(f"{key}: {value}")
```

Q15: How can you sort a list of tuples by the second element?

A15: You can use the sorted() function with a custom sorting key to sort by the second element.

```
my_list = [(1, 'apple'), (3, 'banana'), (2, 'cherry')]
sorted_list = sorted(my_list, key=lambda x: x[1])
print(sorted_list)    # Output: [(1, 'apple'), (3, 'banana'), (2, 'cherry')]
```

Mastering Python's data structures is crucial for acing technical interviews. Understanding how to effectively use **lists**, **tuples**, **dictionaries**, and **sets** can help you solve complex problems quickly and efficiently. The key to performing well in Python interviews is not only knowing these structures but also being able to manipulate them for optimal results. The questions in this chapter will give you a solid foundation for solving coding challenges and impressing interviewers with your Python skills.

As you continue your 30-day interview preparation journey, remember that consistent practice and a deep understanding of Python's core concepts are your best tools for success.

FUNCTIONS, LAMBDAS, AND DECORATORS: A COMPLETE GUIDE

This chapter will focus on advanced function techniques, including **functions**, **lambdas**, and **decorators** in Python. These topics are fundamental to writing clean, efficient, and reusable code. Let's dive straight into the interview questions and their solutions for each of these areas. If you can master these, you'll be able to answer Python interview questions like a pro.

1. What is the difference between a function and a lambda function in Python?

Answer:
A **lambda function** is a small anonymous function, while a **regular function** is defined using the def keyword. Here are the key differences:

- **Syntax**:
  - Regular function: def function_name(args): return value
  - Lambda function: lambda args: value
- **Use Case**:
  Lambda functions are generally used for small operations, like in map(), filter(), or sorted(). They are more concise

but less readable than regular functions for complex operations.

- **Functionality**:
Regular functions can have multiple expressions, while lambda functions can only have a single expression.

Example:

```
# Regular function
def add(x, y):
    return x + y

# Lambda function
add_lambda = lambda x, y: x + y
```

In an interview, you might be asked to implement a small task and told to use a lambda function for simplicity, such as sorting a list of tuples based on the second element.

Example Question:
Sort a list of tuples by the second element using a lambda function.

Solution:

```
data = [(1, 2), (4, 3), (2, 1)]
sorted_data = sorted(data, key=lambda x: x[1])
print(sorted_data)
```

---

2. What are *args and kwargs? How do they work in function definitions?

Answer:

- *args allows a function to accept any number of positional arguments. It is used when you don't know beforehand how many arguments will be passed to your function.
- **kwargs allows a function to accept any number

of keyword arguments. It is used when you don't know beforehand how many keyword arguments will be passed.

Example:

```python
def example(*args, **kwargs):
    print(args)  # Prints the tuple of positional arguments
    print(kwargs) # Prints the dictionary of keyword arguments

example(1, 2, 3, a=4, b=5)
```

Output:

```
(1, 2, 3)
{'a': 4, 'b': 5}
```

In an interview, they might test your understanding of *args and **kwargs by asking you to handle a function that takes an unknown number of inputs.

3. What is a Python decorator, and how do you use it?

Answer:

A **decorator** is a design pattern in Python that allows you to modify the behavior of a function or class. They are often used to wrap another function to extend or alter its behavior. Decorators are implemented using the @decorator_name syntax.

Decorators are commonly used for:

- Logging
- Access control
- Caching
- Validation

How it works:

A decorator is a function that returns another function. The original function is passed to the decorator as an argument and is returned as a modified version of the function.

Example:

```
# Decorator to print the function name before execution
def function_logger(func):
    def wrapper(*args, **kwargs):
        print(f"Function {func.__name__} is called")
        return func(*args, **kwargs)
    return wrapper

@function_logger
def add(x, y):
    return x + y

add(5, 7)
```

Output:

```
Function add is called
```

In an interview, you could be asked to write a decorator that logs the time a function takes to execute, or one that restricts access to a function based on certain conditions.

4. Can you explain closures in Python and provide an example?

Answer:
A **closure** is a function that retains access to the variables from its lexical scope, even after the outer function has finished execution. This allows the inner function to access variables that were in scope when it was created.

Example:

```
def outer_function(x):
    def inner_function(y):
        return x + y
    return inner_function

add_5 = outer_function(5)  # x is now 5
print(add_5(3))  # Output will be 8 (5 + 3)
```

Here, the inner_function is a closure because it remembers the value of x from the outer_function even after outer_function has finished executing.

Interviewers may ask questions related to closures when discussing advanced topics in Python, especially when asking you to design functions with state retention.

5. How can decorators be used with arguments?

Answer:
To use a decorator with arguments, you need an additional layer of function nesting. This is because the decorator itself needs to accept arguments, and it has to return a function that works with the target function.

Example:

```
# Decorator that takes an argument
def repeat(n):
    def decorator(func):
        def wrapper(*args, **kwargs):
            for _ in range(n):
                func(*args, **kwargs)
        return wrapper
    return decorator

@repeat(3)
def greet(name):
```

```
    print(f"Hello, {name}!")

greet("John")
```

Output:

Hello, John!
Hello, John!
Hello, John!

In this example, the repeat decorator takes a parameter n, which determines how many times the function greet will be called. This type of decorator is useful in scenarios like retry logic or repeating an action multiple times.

6. What is the difference between a function with a return value and a function with no return value in Python?

Answer:

- A **function with a return value** explicitly uses the return statement to return a value to the caller.
- A **function with no return value** simply executes its code and exits. If no return statement is provided, Python automatically returns None.

Example:

```
# Function with a return value
def multiply(x, y):
    return x * y

# Function with no return value
def print_message(message):
    print(message)

result = multiply(5, 10)  # result will hold the value 50
```

print_message("Hello!")   # No return value, just prints the message

In an interview, you may be asked to explain the behavior of functions that return a value vs. those that don't, especially in the context of larger codebases where understanding side effects is crucial.

7. What is the use of the functools.wraps() method in decorators?

Answer:
The functools.wraps() method is used to preserve the metadata (like the name, docstring, etc.) of the original function when it is wrapped by a decorator. Without this, the wrapped function may lose its original properties.

Example:

```python
import functools

def decorator(func):
    @functools.wraps(func) # Preserves metadata
    def wrapper(*args, **kwargs):
        print("Before function call")
        return func(*args, **kwargs)
    return wrapper

@decorator
def sample_function():
    """This is a sample function"""
    print("Inside function")

print(sample_function.__name__)       # Output will be
'sample_function'
```

Without wraps(), sample_function.__name__ **would return**

wrapper, which can cause confusion. Interviewers may test your understanding of this when asking you to implement decorators or logging systems.

8. How would you use a decorator to memoize a function in Python?

Answer:
Memoization is a technique where you store the results of expensive function calls and reuse the result when the same inputs occur again. Python's functools.lru_cache decorator is typically used for this.

Example:

```
from functools import lru_cache

@lru_cache(maxsize=None) # No limit on cache size
def expensive_computation(n):
    if n <= 1:
        return 1
    return n * expensive_computation(n - 1)

print(expensive_computation(10))
```

The @lru_cache decorator caches the results of previous calls to expensive_computation(), making subsequent calls with the same argument much faster. This type of decorator can be a common interview question when discussing performance optimization.

Mastering **functions, lambdas, and decorators** is key to excelling in Python interviews. By practicing these advanced topics, you can not only showcase your ability to write efficient and reusable code, but also demonstrate a deeper understanding of Python's core principles. These questions and answers will help you ace your interview by preparing you for common scenarios where you might need to implement and explain these techniques.

CLASSES AND OBJECTS: THE OOP JOURNEY

1. What is Object-Oriented Programming (OOP)?

Answer:
Object-Oriented Programming (OOP) is a programming paradigm based on the concept of "objects." These objects are instances of classes, which are blueprints for the objects. The four main principles of OOP are:

- **Encapsulation**: Bundling data and methods into a single unit, the class.
- **Abstraction**: Hiding the complexity and showing only the essential features.
- **Inheritance**: The ability of a class to inherit properties and methods from another class.
- **Polymorphism**: The ability of different classes to respond to the same method call in different ways.

2. What is a class in Python?

Answer:
A class in Python is a blueprint for creating objects. It defines attributes (data members) and methods (functions) that the created objects will have. A class is defined using the class keyword.

```python
class Car:
    def __init__(self, model, color):
        self.model = model
        self.color = color

    def display_info(self):
        print(f"Model: {self.model}, Color: {self.color}")

# Example of creating an object of the class
car1 = Car("Tesla", "Red")
car1.display_info()  # Output: Model: Tesla, Color: Red
```

3. What is the purpose of the __init__() method in a class?

Answer:
The __init__() method is the constructor method in Python. It is automatically called when an object of the class is instantiated. It is used to initialize the attributes of the object.

```python
class Person:
    def __init__(self, name, age):
        self.name = name
        self.age = age


p1 = Person("John", 30)  # __init__ method is automatically called
```

4. What is the difference between self and cls in Python classes?

Answer:

- self refers to the instance of the class. It is used to access instance attributes and methods within the class.
- cls refers to the class itself and is used in class methods to access class-level variables and methods.

Example:

```python
class Example:
    count = 0  # Class variable

    def __init__(self, value):
        self.value = value
        Example.count += 1  # Accessing class variable using class name

    @classmethod
    def show_count(cls):
        print("Total objects:", cls.count)  # Using 'cls' to access class variable

obj1 = Example(10)
obj2 = Example(20)
Example.show_count()  # Output: Total objects: 2
```

5. What is inheritance in Python?

Answer:
Inheritance allows a class (child class) to inherit methods and attributes from another class (parent class). It promotes code reusability and is a key feature of OOP.

```python
class Animal:
    def sound(self):
        print("Animal makes a sound")

class Dog(Animal):
    def sound(self):
        print("Dog barks")

d = Dog()
d.sound()  # Output: Dog barks
```

6. What is method overriding in Python?

Answer:
Method overriding occurs when a subclass defines a method that already exists in its superclass with the same signature. The subclass's method will override the parent class's method.

```python
class Parent:
    def greet(self):
```

```
    print("Hello from Parent")


class Child(Parent):
    def greet(self):
        print("Hello from Child")


c = Child()
c.greet()  # Output: Hello from Child
```

7. What is the difference between @staticmethod and @classmethod in Python?

Answer:

- **@staticmethod**: A static method does not take self or cls as its first argument. It behaves like a regular function but belongs to the class's namespace. It cannot access or modify class or instance-specific data.
- **@classmethod**: A class method takes cls as its first argument and can modify class-level variables. It is used to access and modify class state.

Example:

```
class Example:
    count = 0


    def __init__(self):
        Example.count += 1
```

```python
@staticmethod
def static_method():
    print("This is a static method")


@classmethod
def class_method(cls):
    print(f"This is a class method. Count: {cls.count}")


Example.static_method()  # Output: This is a static method
Example.class_method()    # Output: This is a class method.
Count: 0
```

8. What is encapsulation in Python?

Answer:
Encapsulation is the concept of bundling data (attributes) and methods (functions) that operate on the data within a single unit, the class. It also involves restricting access to some of an object's components, which is usually done through private variables and methods.

```python
class BankAccount:
    def __init__(self, balance):
        self.__balance = balance  # Private variable


    def deposit(self, amount):
```

```python
    if amount > 0:
        self.__balance += amount

    def get_balance(self):
        return self.__balance

account = BankAccount(1000)
account.deposit(500)
print(account.get_balance())  # Output: 1500
```

Here, __balance is a private attribute and cannot be accessed directly outside the class.

9. What is polymorphism in Python?

Answer:
Polymorphism allows objects of different classes to be treated as objects of a common superclass. The actual method that gets called is determined at runtime based on the object's type.

```python
class Bird:
    def sound(self):
        print("Chirp")


class Dog:
    def sound(self):
        print("Bark")
```

```python
def make_sound(animal):
    animal.sound()


b = Bird()
d = Dog()
make_sound(b)  # Output: Chirp
make_sound(d)  # Output: Bark
```

10. What is the difference between is and == in Python?

Answer:

- is checks if two references point to the same object in memory (identity comparison).
- == checks if the values of two objects are equal (value comparison).

Example:

```python
a = [1, 2, 3]
b = [1, 2, 3]
c = a


print(a == b)  # Output: True (values are the same)
print(a is b)  # Output: False (different objects in memory)
print(a is c)  # Output: True (both refer to the same object)
```

11. What is the super() function in Python?

Answer:
The super() function is used to call methods from a parent class in a child class. It is commonly used in the constructor to initialize the parent class.

```python
class Animal:
    def __init__(self, name):
        self.name = name


class Dog(Animal):
    def __init__(self, name, breed):
        super().__init__(name)
        self.breed = breed


d = Dog("Buddy", "Golden Retriever")
print(d.name)  # Output: Buddy
print(d.breed) # Output: Golden Retriever
```

12. What is an abstract class in Python?

Answer:
An abstract class is a class that cannot be instantiated directly. It serves as a blueprint for other classes. Abstract methods defined in an abstract class must be implemented by any subclass.

```python
from abc import ABC, abstractmethod

class Animal(ABC):
    @abstractmethod
    def sound(self):
        pass

class Dog(Animal):
    def sound(self):
        print("Bark")

d = Dog()
d.sound()  # Output: Bark
```

13. What is multiple inheritance in Python?

Answer:
Multiple inheritance is when a class can inherit from more than one parent class. Python supports multiple inheritance, unlike some other programming languages.

```python
class A:
    def method_A(self):
        print("Method of class A")
```

```
class B:
    def method_B(self):
        print("Method of class B")


class C(A, B):
    def method_C(self):
        print("Method of class C")


c = C()
c.method_A()  # Output: Method of class A
c.method_B()  # Output: Method of class B
c.method_C()  # Output: Method of class C
```

14. What is the __del__() method in Python?

Answer:
The __del__() method is the destructor method in Python. It is called when an object is about to be destroyed (i.e., when the object's reference count reaches zero).

```
class Test:
    def __del__(self):
        print("Object is being deleted")
t = Test()
del t
```

FILE HANDLING AND DATA MANAGEMENT

In Python, file handling is an essential skill for many interview questions, especially when the job role involves data manipulation, automation, or working with external data sources. This chapter is dedicated to Python's file handling capabilities—how to read, write, and manage data files effectively.

Below are some of the most common file-handling interview questions along with their answers.

1. How do you open a file in Python?

Answer: To open a file in Python, use the built-in open() function. This function returns a file object, which you can use to interact with the file.

Example:

```python
file = open('example.txt', 'r')
```

The open() function takes two arguments:

- The file path ('example.txt' in this case).
- The mode ('r' for reading, 'w' for writing, 'a' for appending, etc.).

Other common modes include:

- 'r': Read (default mode).
- 'w': Write (creates the file if it doesn't exist).
- 'a': Append.
- 'b': Binary mode (for non-text files).

You can also use the with statement to automatically close the file after use:

```
with open('example.txt', 'r') as file:
    content = file.read()
```

This ensures that the file is properly closed, even if an exception occurs.

2. How do you read from a file in Python?

Answer: You can read from a file using methods like read(), readline(), and readlines().

read(): Reads the entire file.

```
with open('example.txt', 'r') as file:
    content = file.read()
```

-

readline(): Reads one line at a time. This is useful for iterating over lines in a file.

```
with open('example.txt', 'r') as file:
    line = file.readline()
```

-

readlines(): Reads all lines into a list. Each line is a string in the list.

```
with open('example.txt', 'r') as file:
    lines = file.readlines()
```
-

---

3. How do you write to a file in Python?

Answer: You can write to a file using write() or writelines() methods.

write(): Writes a string to the file. If the file already exists, it will be overwritten unless the mode is set to append ('a').

```
with open('example.txt', 'w') as file:
    file.write('Hello, World!')
```
-

writelines(): Writes a list of strings to the file. Each string is written on the same line.

```
with open('example.txt', 'w') as file:
    file.writelines(['Hello', 'World', 'Python'])
```
-

---

4. How do you append data to an existing file in Python?

Answer: To append data to an existing file without overwriting it, open the file in append mode ('a').

Example:

```
with open('example.txt', 'a') as file:
    file.write('This will be appended.')
```

This ensures that the data is added to the end of the file, leaving the existing contents intact.

5. How can you delete a file in Python?

Answer: You can use the os.remove() method to delete a file.

Example:

```
import os
os.remove('example.txt')
```

Ensure that the file exists before trying to delete it, as attempting to delete a non-existent file will raise an error.

6. How do you handle exceptions while working with files in Python?

Answer: When handling files, it's important to manage potential exceptions such as FileNotFoundError, PermissionError, etc. You can use try and except blocks to handle these errors gracefully.

Example:

```
try:
    with open('example.txt', 'r') as file:
        content = file.read()
except FileNotFoundError:
    print("File not found.")
```

except PermissionError:

  print("Permission denied.")

This allows the program to continue running smoothly even if an error occurs during file handling.

7. What are the different modes for opening a file in Python?

Answer: The open() function in Python supports several modes to specify how a file should be handled:

- 'r': Read (default mode). Opens the file for reading.
- 'w': Write. Opens the file for writing (creates the file if it doesn't exist).
- 'a': Append. Opens the file for appending data (creates the file if it doesn't exist).
- 'b': Binary mode. Used for reading or writing binary files (e.g., images, audio files).
- 'x': Exclusive creation. Creates a new file, but if the file already exists, it raises a FileExistsError.
- 't': Text mode. (Default mode for text files; it is usually not specified).
- 'U': Universal newline mode. This allows for reading files with different line-ending conventions.

8. What is the difference between read() and readlines()?

Answer:

read(): Reads the entire file into a single string. This is efficient for small files.

with open('example.txt', 'r') as file:

```
content = file.read()
```

●

readlines(): Reads all lines in a file into a list. Each line becomes an item in the list, which is useful when you need to process each line individually.

```
with open('example.txt', 'r') as file:
    lines = file.readlines()
```

●

---

9. How do you manage large files (e.g., log files) in Python?

Answer: For handling large files efficiently, avoid reading the entire file at once (which could consume too much memory). Instead, read the file line by line.

Example:

```
with open('large_file.txt', 'r') as file:
    for line in file:
        process(line) # Replace with your processing function
```

This approach helps manage memory usage effectively, especially when dealing with large datasets.

---

10. How do you check if a file exists before opening it in Python?

Answer: You can use the os.path.exists() method or os.path.isfile() to check if a file exists before attempting to open it.

Example:

```
import os

if os.path.exists('example.txt'):
    with open('example.txt', 'r') as file:
        content = file.read()
else:
    print("File does not exist.")
```

11. How do you write data in binary format in Python?

Answer: When dealing with non-text data, you need to open the file in binary mode ('wb' or 'rb').

Example for writing binary data:

```
data = b"Hello, binary world!"  # b before string indicates binary data
with open('example.bin', 'wb') as file:
    file.write(data)
```

For reading binary data:

```
with open('example.bin', 'rb') as file:
    data = file.read()
```

```
print(data)
```

---

12. What is the use of seek() and tell() functions in file handling?

Answer:

seek(offset, whence): Moves the file pointer to a specified position in the file. offset is the number of bytes, and whence defines the reference point (default is os.SEEK_SET, which means the start of the file).

file.seek(0) # Moves to the beginning of the file

-

tell(): Returns the current position of the file pointer.

position = file.tell() # Returns the current position in the file

-

In this chapter, we covered essential file handling techniques in Python, including opening, reading, writing, appending, deleting files, and handling exceptions. Mastering these skills is vital for answering file manipulation questions in interviews. Make sure to practice each of these concepts, as they form the foundation of real-world Python applications, especially when dealing with data files.

HANDLING ERRORS LIKE A PRO

In the fast-paced environment of coding interviews, being able to debug code efficiently and handle errors gracefully is a crucial skill. This chapter will focus on the most commonly asked questions related to error handling and debugging in Python, as well as the best approaches to solve real-time challenges during interviews. We'll dive into key concepts like exceptions, error handling mechanisms, and best practices, but without going into unnecessary theory—just the essential interview-ready knowledge.

Q1: What are exceptions in Python? How do you handle them?

Answer: An exception in Python is an event that disrupts the normal flow of a program. It occurs when the Python interpreter encounters an error during the program execution. If exceptions are not handled, they will terminate the program.

In Python, exceptions can be handled using the try, except block.

Here's the syntax:

```
try:
    # Code that might raise an exception
except ExceptionType as e:
    # Handling the exception
    print(f"An error occurred: {e}")
```

Example:

```
try:
    num = int(input("Enter a number: "))
    result = 10 / num
except ValueError:
    print("Invalid input! Please enter a valid number.")
except ZeroDivisionError:
    print("Error! Division by zero is not allowed.")
```

Explanation:

- ValueError handles cases where the input is not a valid number.
- ZeroDivisionError handles the case where the user tries to divide by zero.

In interviews, you might be asked to handle multiple exceptions in one block, or to handle a specific error that occurs in certain operations (like file reading, or network requests). Always ensure you catch the specific error before using a general except.

Q2: What is the difference between try/except and try/finally?

Answer:

- try/except is used for handling exceptions—catching errors when they occur.
- try/finally is used for ensuring that some code runs no matter what, whether an exception occurs or not.

try/finally is typically used for cleanup operations, like closing files or releasing resources.

Example:

```
try:
```

```
file = open("data.txt", "r")
# Perform operations with file
finally:
    file.close()  # This will always execute, even if an exception
occurs
```

Explanation: In this case, whether an exception occurs or not, the finally block will close the file to prevent resource leakage. This is especially useful in situations where it's critical to release resources like file handles, network connections, etc.

Q3: How would you raise an exception in Python?

Answer: In Python, you can raise exceptions explicitly using the raise keyword. This can be useful if you want to create custom error messages or handle errors in a specific way.

Syntax:

```
raise Exception("Custom error message")
```

Example:

```
def check_age(age):
    if age < 18:
        raise ValueError("Age must be 18 or older!")
    return age
```

Explanation: In this example, if the user provides an age less than 18, a ValueError is raised with a custom message. You can raise built-in exceptions like ValueError, TypeError, or even custom exceptions if needed.

Q4: What is the purpose of else in a try/except block?

Answer: The else block is executed if no exceptions were raised in the try block. It's used for code that should run only when no errors occurred.

Example:

```
try:
    number = int(input("Enter a number: "))
    result = 10 / number
except ZeroDivisionError:
    print("Cannot divide by zero!")
else:
    print(f"Result: {result}")
```

Explanation:

- If the user enters a valid number and doesn't cause any exceptions, the else block will execute, printing the result.
- If there's a ZeroDivisionError or any other exception, the else block is skipped.

Q5: How do you handle multiple exceptions in Python?

Answer: You can handle multiple exceptions by using multiple except blocks. Alternatively, you can catch multiple exceptions in a single block using a tuple.

Example (Multiple except blocks):

```
try:
    # Some code
except ValueError:
    print("ValueError occurred")
except ZeroDivisionError:
    print("ZeroDivisionError occurred")
```

Example (Single except block with multiple exceptions):

```
try:
    # Some code
except (ValueError, ZeroDivisionError) as e:
    print(f"Error: {e}")
```

Explanation:

- In the first approach, each error type is handled separately.
- In the second approach, we handle multiple error types in one block, which is concise and efficient.

Q6: What is the assert statement and when would you use it?

Answer: The assert statement is used for debugging purposes. It tests if a condition is True, and if not, it raises an AssertionError.

Syntax:

```
assert condition, "Error message"
```

Example:

```
def divide(x, y):
    assert y != 0, "Division by zero is not allowed!"
    return x / y
```

Explanation:

- The assert statement checks if the divisor (y) is not zero. If it is, the program raises an AssertionError with the message "Division by zero is not allowed!"

Note: assert is mainly used during development and debugging. It's usually disabled in optimized mode (when running with the -O flag), so it's not intended for runtime error handling.

Q7: What is the difference between IndexError and KeyError?

Answer:

- IndexError occurs when you try to access an index in a list that doesn't exist.
- KeyError occurs when you try to access a dictionary with a key that doesn't exist.

Example of IndexError:

```
my_list = [1, 2, 3]
print(my_list[5])  # IndexError: list index out of range
```

Example of KeyError:

```
my_dict = {"name": "Alice", "age": 25}
print(my_dict["address"])  # KeyError: 'address'
```

Explanation:

- In the first example, the index 5 doesn't exist in the list, so an IndexError is raised.
- In the second example, the key 'address' doesn't exist in the dictionary, resulting in a KeyError.

Q8: What are custom exceptions in Python?

Answer: Custom exceptions allow you to define your own exceptions that are specific to your program's needs. You create a custom exception by subclassing the built-in Exception class.

Syntax:

```
class CustomError(Exception):
    pass
```

Example:

```
class NegativeNumberError(Exception):
    def __init__(self, message="Negative numbers are not
allowed"):
        self.message = message
        super().__init__(self.message)

def check_number(num):
    if num < 0:
        raise NegativeNumberError
    return num
```

Explanation:

- The NegativeNumberError is a custom exception. When the function check_number receives a negative number, it raises this custom exception.

Q9: How do you log exceptions in Python?

Answer: Python's logging module provides a flexible way to log information, including exceptions.

Example:

```
import logging

logging.basicConfig(filename='app.log', level=logging.ERROR)

try:
    num = 10 / 0
except ZeroDivisionError as e:
    logging.error(f"Error occurred: {e}")
```

Explanation:

- The logging.error() function logs the error message to a log file (app.log).

- This is especially useful in real-world applications where you need to track errors and debug efficiently.

Mastering error handling and debugging in Python is not just about knowing the syntax but also about understanding how to approach problems efficiently. In Python interviews, demonstrating that you can handle real-world issues, such as exceptions and debugging, will set you apart. By practicing the scenarios above, you can handle almost any exception scenario that comes your way in a Python interview.

PYTHON'S MAGIC: GENERATORS, ITERATORS, AND CONTEXT MANAGERS

Python is a powerful language, and its advanced constructs—such as **generators**, **iterators**, and **context managers**—enable developers to write cleaner, more efficient code. These features are often used in technical interviews, and mastering them is essential to answering questions like a pro. In this chapter, we'll focus on how to use these features in Python interviews, covering the most frequently asked questions and providing expert-level answers that will help you stand out.

1. What is a Generator in Python?

Question: What is a generator, and how does it differ from a normal function?

Answer:

A **generator** is a special type of iterator that is defined using a function, but it uses the yield keyword to return values. Instead of returning a single value and terminating, a generator can yield multiple values one at a time, pausing the function's state between each yield. This makes generators memory-efficient when working with large data sets because they do not need to store all items in memory at once.

Example:

```
def count_up_to(limit):

    count = 1

    while count <= limit:

        yield count

        count += 1
```

Explanation: Here, the count_up_to function is a generator that yields numbers one by one, from 1 up to the specified limit. When the generator function is called, it does not run immediately; instead, it returns a generator object.

Usage:

```
gen = count_up_to(5)

for number in gen:

    print(number)
```

This will output:

1

2

3

4

5

Key Points for Interviews:

- **Memory Efficiency:** Generators are memory-efficient because they don't store the entire sequence in memory. Instead, they generate each item on-the-fly.
- **Performance:** Generators can improve performance when working with large datasets or infinite sequences.

---

2. What is the Difference Between a Generator and a List?

Question: How is a generator different from a list? What are the advantages?

Answer:

A **list** in Python stores all elements in memory, meaning if you have a large list, it can consume a lot of memory. In contrast, a **generator** computes each item only when needed and does not store the entire sequence in memory. This is especially useful when dealing with large datasets or when you only need to iterate through data once.

Example:

```
# Using a List

my_list = [x * 2 for x in range(1000000)]


# Using a Generator

my_gen = (x * 2 for x in range(1000000))
```

Key Differences:

1. **Memory Usage:**
   - Lists hold all values in memory.
   - Generators compute values one at a time, reducing memory consumption.
2. **Performance:**
   - Lists can be faster for random access, as elements are stored in memory.
   - Generators excel in scenarios where you only need sequential access.

Interview Tip: Be prepared to explain how generators can be more efficient for specific scenarios, such as handling large files or streaming data.

3. What is an Iterator?

Question: What is an iterator in Python, and

how is it related to generators?

Answer:

An **iterator** is an object in Python that implements two methods: __iter__() and __next__(). These methods allow an object to be traversed (i.e., iterated over) in a loop, such as in a for loop. While all generators are iterators, not all iterators are generators.

- __iter__() returns the iterator object itself.
- __next__() returns the next item from the collection. When there are no more items, it raises a StopIteration exception.

Example of an Iterator:

```python
class Reverse:
    def __init__(self, data):
        self.data = data
        self.index = len(data)

    def __iter__(self):
        return self

    def __next__(self):
        if self.index == 0:
```

```
        raise StopIteration

    self.index = self.index - 1

    return self.data[self.index]


rev = Reverse('giraffe')

for char in rev:

    print(char)
```

Explanation: The Reverse class implements an iterator that goes through a string in reverse order. This iterator can be used in a for loop.

Key Interview Points:

- **Generators** are a simpler, more concise way to create iterators.
- Any object that implements the __iter__() and __next__() methods is an iterator.

---

4. What is the yield Keyword?

Question: What is the yield keyword, and why is it important in generators?

Answer:

The yield keyword is what makes a function a generator. It

pauses the function's execution and returns a value to the caller, but retains the state of the function. The next time next() is called, the function resumes execution right after the yield statement.

Example:

```
def fibonacci(n):

    a, b = 0, 1

    for _ in range(n):

        yield a

        a, b = b, a + b
```

Explanation: This generator yields the Fibonacci sequence up to the nth term. The function doesn't compute the entire sequence upfront, making it memory efficient. Each time next() is called on the generator, it yields the next Fibonacci number.

Key Interview Points:

- The **yield** statement is used to create **lazy iterators** (i.e., generators).
- **Memory Efficiency:** Unlike a return statement, yield allows you to work with potentially infinite sequences or large datasets without consuming memory.

5. What are Context Managers and the with Statement?

Question: What is a context manager in Python, and how is it used with the with statement?

Answer:

A **context manager** in Python is used to manage resources like files, network connections, or locks. It ensures that resources are properly acquired and released, even if an exception occurs within the block of code.

The with **statement** is used to simplify working with context managers. It automatically handles resource management, such as opening and closing files.

Example:

```
with open('my_file.txt', 'r') as file:

    content = file.read()

    print(content)
```

Explanation: The with statement ensures that the file is opened and closed properly. If an exception occurs inside the block, the context manager ensures that the file is still closed.

Key Interview Points:

- **Context Managers** are commonly used for resource management like file handling, database connections, etc.
- The __enter__() and __exit__() methods define how the resource is managed.

Custom Context Manager Example:

```python
class MyContextManager:

    def __enter__(self):

        print("Resource acquired")

        return self


    def __exit__(self, exc_type, exc_val, exc_tb):

        print("Resource released")


with MyContextManager() as manager:

    print("Using the resource")
```

Output:

Resource acquired

Using the resource

Resource released

---

6. How Do Generators and Context

Managers Work Together?

Question: Can generators and context managers be combined in a Python program? How does it benefit resource management?

Answer:

Yes, you can combine **generators** and **context managers** to handle resource management efficiently while generating data on-the-fly. A context manager can be used to manage the setup and teardown of a resource, while a generator can yield values from that resource.

Example:

```python
class FileGenerator:

    def __init__(self, filename):

        self.filename = filename


    def __enter__(self):

        self.file = open(self.filename, 'r')

        return self


    def __exit__(self, exc_type, exc_val, exc_tb):

        self.file.close()
```

```
def read_lines(self):

    for line in self.file:

        yield line.strip()


with FileGenerator('sample.txt') as file_gen:

    for line in file_gen.read_lines():

        print(line)
```

Explanation: Here, the FileGenerator class combines both generator behavior (yielding lines from a file) and context management (ensuring the file is opened and closed properly).

Key Interview Point:

- Combining **generators** and **context managers** makes it easy to handle resources that require cleanup, such as reading from a file or connecting to a database.

---

7. What is the Purpose of __enter__() and __exit__() Methods in a Context Manager?

Question: What role do the __enter__() and __exit__() methods play in a context manager?

Answer:

- The __enter__() method is executed when the with block is entered, and it typically returns the resource to be used.
- The __exit__() method is executed when the block is exited, whether normally or via an exception, and it handles cleanup tasks, such as closing files or releasing locks.

Mastering **generators**, **iterators**, and **context managers** in Python can significantly improve the quality and performance of your code. These constructs are not only memory-efficient but also enhance readability and reusability. In Python interviews, these advanced concepts are often asked to test your problem-solving abilities and understanding of the language. Understanding how and when to use these features is crucial for showcasing your expertise and impressing interviewers.

By implementing these techniques effectively, you demonstrate not only a deep knowledge of Python but also the ability to write high-quality, maintainable code—qualities that are highly valued by employers.

THE POWER OF LIBRARIES

In Python programming, libraries play a significant role in simplifying complex tasks. Rather than reinventing the wheel, you can use these libraries to perform complex operations efficiently. As a Python developer, understanding the most widely used libraries is crucial, especially during interviews. In this chapter, we'll cover three of the most important Python libraries: **Pandas**, **NumPy**, and **Matplotlib**. These libraries are frequently tested in interviews, especially for roles involving data analysis, data science, and machine learning.

1. Pandas

What is Pandas?

Pandas is an open-source data analysis and manipulation library that provides data structures like DataFrame and Series to work with structured data. It is a go-to library for working with data tables and time-series data. Pandas allows you to clean, filter, transform, and analyze data in an efficient and easy-to-read format.

Interview Question 1: What is the difference between a Pandas DataFrame and Series?

A **DataFrame** is a two-dimensional, size-mutable, potentially heterogeneous tabular data structure, while a **Series** is a one-dimensional array-like object. A DataFrame consists of rows and columns, whereas a Series is essentially a single column. A DataFrame can contain multiple Series.

Interview Question 2: How would you handle missing data in Pandas?

To handle missing data in Pandas, you can use the following methods:

- dropna(): This method removes missing values (NaN) from the DataFrame.
- fillna(): You can fill missing values with a specified value or forward/backward fill.
- isna(): This function checks for missing data in a DataFrame or Series.

Example:

```
import pandas as pd
df = pd.DataFrame({'A': [1, 2, None, 4], 'B': [None, 2, 3, 4]})
df.fillna(0)  # Replaces NaN with 0
```

Interview Question 3: How do you merge two DataFrames in Pandas?

Pandas provides the merge() function to merge DataFrames, similar to SQL joins. You can merge on a column or index. The most commonly used merge types are inner, left, right, and outer.

Example:

```
df1 = pd.DataFrame({'key': ['A', 'B', 'C'], 'value': [1, 2, 3]})
df2 = pd.DataFrame({'key': ['B', 'C', 'D'], 'value': [4, 5, 6]})
merged_df = pd.merge(df1, df2, on='key', how='inner')
```

2. NumPy

What is NumPy?

NumPy is a powerful library for numerical computing in Python. It provides support for large, multi-dimensional arrays and matrices, along with a wide collection of high-level mathematical functions to operate on these arrays. It is fundamental for scientific computing and is heavily used in data science and machine learning.

Interview Question 1: What are the advantages of using NumPy arrays over Python lists?

NumPy arrays offer several advantages:

- **Faster performance**: NumPy arrays are more efficient in memory and faster in processing than Python lists.
- **Vectorized operations**: You can perform element-wise operations on NumPy arrays without using loops, which is much faster.
- **Multi-dimensional arrays**: NumPy supports arrays with more than one dimension (like matrices), whereas Python lists are one-dimensional.

Example:

```
import numpy as np
arr = np.array([1, 2, 3])
arr + 2  # Element-wise addition
```

Interview Question 2: How do you create a NumPy array from a Python list?

You can easily convert a Python list to a NumPy array using np.array().

Example:

```
python_list = [1, 2, 3, 4]
numpy_array = np.array(python_list)
```

Interview Question 3: How would you find the mean, median, and standard deviation of a NumPy array?
NumPy provides built-in functions to calculate statistical measures.

- **np.mean()**: Calculates the mean (average) of the array.
- **np.median()**: Finds the median of the array.
- **np.std()**: Computes the standard deviation.

Example:

```
arr = np.array([1, 2, 3, 4, 5])
mean = np.mean(arr)
median = np.median(arr)
std_dev = np.std(arr)
```

3. Matplotlib

What is Matplotlib?
Matplotlib is a plotting library for creating static, animated, and interactive visualizations in Python. It is widely used for generating graphs, charts, and plots from data, making it essential for data analysts and scientists during Python interviews.

Interview Question 1: How would you plot a simple line graph using Matplotlib?
You can create a simple line plot by using plt.plot() and then

showing the plot with **plt.show()**.

Example:

```
import matplotlib.pyplot as plt

x = [1, 2, 3, 4, 5]
y = [1, 4, 9, 16, 25]

plt.plot(x, y)
plt.title("Simple Line Graph")
plt.xlabel("X Axis")
plt.ylabel("Y Axis")
plt.show()
```

Interview Question 2: How do you create a bar chart in Matplotlib?
A bar chart can be created using **plt.bar()**.

Example:

```
categories = ['A', 'B', 'C', 'D']
values = [10, 20, 30, 40]

plt.bar(categories, values)
plt.title("Bar Chart")
plt.xlabel("Categories")
```

```
plt.ylabel("Values")

plt.show()
```

Interview Question 3: How do you customize a plot's appearance in Matplotlib?

You can customize the appearance by modifying the figure, axis labels, title, line styles, and more using various Matplotlib functions. For example, you can change the line style, color, and markers.

Example:

```
plt.plot(x, y, color='red', linestyle='--', marker='o')

plt.title("Customized Line Plot")

plt.xlabel("X Axis")

plt.ylabel("Y Axis")

plt.grid(True)

plt.show()
```

Mastering libraries like Pandas, NumPy, and Matplotlib will significantly boost your performance in Python interviews, especially for roles related to data science, machine learning, and general software development. These libraries are designed to save time and increase efficiency, which is why they are regularly featured in interviews for technical positions. Understanding the key functionalities and how to answer common interview questions related to these libraries will set you apart from the competition.

Make sure to practice coding examples and solutions for the

most commonly asked questions from Pandas, NumPy, and Matplotlib. This will not only increase your chances of success in the interview but will also enhance your Python programming skills overall.

DECORATORS, METACLASSES, AND PYTHON INTERNALS

In Python, decorators, metaclasses, and internal workings of the language represent powerful tools that can elevate your coding proficiency and demonstrate advanced knowledge during an interview. This chapter dives into these advanced Python concepts with practical examples and insights into their real-world applications, focusing on interview-ready questions and answers.

1. What is a Python Decorator?

Question: *What is a decorator in Python, and how is it used?*

Answer:

A **decorator** in Python is a design pattern that allows a function or method to be dynamically modified or extended without changing its source code. It is implemented using the @decorator_name syntax placed above a function definition. A decorator takes a function as input and returns a modified function.

Here is an example:

```
def decorator_function(func):
    def wrapper():
```

```
        print("Before function call")
        func()
        print("After function call")
    return wrapper


@decorator_function
def say_hello():
    print("Hello, World!")


say_hello()
```

Output:

Before function call

Hello, World!

After function call

- **Explanation**: The @decorator_function is applied to say_hello, which allows additional behavior (the print statements) to be added before and after the original function runs. This is particularly useful when you need to extend or modify functions in a consistent and reusable way.

2. What Are Some Common Use Cases for Decorators in Python?

Question: *What are some real-world applications of decorators?*

Answer:

Decorators are widely used in various scenarios:

- **Logging**: Track function execution without modifying the function body.
- **Authorization**: Check user permissions before allowing a function to execute (e.g., user authentication in web frameworks like Flask or Django).
- **Memoization/Caching**: Store results of expensive function calls for later use to improve performance (e.g., using functools.lru_cache).
- **Enrichment**: Modify or enhance the data returned by functions.

Example: Caching a function result using functools.lru_cache:

```python
from functools import lru_cache


@lru_cache(maxsize=100)
def expensive_function(n):
    print("Calculating...")
    return n * n


print(expensive_function(4))
print(expensive_function(4)) # Result cached
```

Output:

```
Calculating...
16
16
```

- **Explanation**: The decorator caches the result of the expensive function call and avoids recalculating it when the same argument is passed again.

---

3. What is the Purpose of Metaclasses in Python?

Question: *What is a metaclass in Python, and how does it work?*

Answer:
A **metaclass** in Python is a class of a class. It defines how classes themselves are constructed and behaves. Metaclasses allow you to customize class creation and modify class attributes dynamically. The most common use case of metaclasses is to control the behavior of class instantiation and inheritance.

In Python, classes are instantiated using the type() function, which is also a metaclass. For example:

```python
class MyClass:

    pass


# Checking the metaclass
print(type(MyClass)) # <class 'type'>
```

You can define your own metaclass to intercept the creation of classes, modify their attributes, or add new methods.

Example: A metaclass that automatically adds a greet method to every class it creates:

```python
class GreetMeta(type):
```

```
def __new__(cls, name, bases, dct):

    dct['greet'] = lambda self: "Hello from " +
self.__class__.__name__

    return super().__new__(cls, name, bases, dct)


class Person(metaclass=GreetMeta):

    pass


p = Person()

print(p.greet()) # Output: Hello from Person
```

- **Explanation**: The GreetMeta metaclass modifies the Person class to include a greet method, demonstrating how metaclasses can dynamically influence class behavior.

---

4. How Are Metaclasses Used in Python Frameworks?

Question: *How are metaclasses used in Python frameworks, such as Django?*

Answer:
In frameworks like **Django**, metaclasses are used to dynamically create classes that behave according to specific rules. For example, Django's **Model** class, which represents a database table, is created using a metaclass. This metaclass allows the model class to automatically map its attributes to database columns without the need for manual configuration.

Django's Model class is defined using a custom metaclass that interacts with its database system to create tables, define relationships, and manage migrations. Here's a simplified example:

```
class MyModelMeta(type):
    def __new__(cls, name, bases, dct):
        dct['table_name'] = name.lower()  # Automatically name the table after the class name
        return super().__new__(cls, name, bases, dct)


class MyModel(metaclass=MyModelMeta):
    pass


print(MyModel.table_name) # Output: mymodel
```

- **Explanation**: The metaclass automatically sets the table_name attribute based on the class name, mimicking Django's behavior of automatically creating tables in the database based on model class names.

5. What Are Python Internals?

Question: *What are the key Python internals you should know for an interview?*

Answer:
Understanding Python internals helps you appreciate the mechanics behind Python's performance, memory management, and how the language executes your code. Some important Python internals include:

- **Memory Management**: Python uses an automatic garbage collection mechanism, which means the interpreter automatically reclaims memory by deleting objects that are no longer in use.

- **Reference Counting**: Every object in Python has a reference count that tracks how many references point to that object.
- **Global Interpreter Lock (GIL)**: Python's GIL prevents multiple threads from executing Python bytecodes in parallel. Understanding this limitation is crucial for multithreading in Python.
- **Bytecode**: Python code is compiled into bytecode, which is then interpreted by the Python virtual machine (PVM). This is how Python manages to execute code across different platforms.

Example of reference counting:

```
import sys

a = [1, 2, 3]
print(sys.getrefcount(a))  # Output: 2 (one for 'a' and one for sys.getrefcount)
```

- **Explanation**: The sys.getrefcount() function returns the reference count for an object, which is useful for understanding Python's memory management.

---

6. How Does Python Handle Object Instantiation?

Question: *How does Python handle object instantiation internally?*

Answer:
Python handles object instantiation through its __new__ and __init__ methods.

- __new__: This method is responsible for creating a new instance of a class. It returns a new object.

- __init__: After the object is created, __init__ initializes the object's state.

Here's an example of both methods in action:

```
class MyClass:
    def __new__(cls):
        print("Creating a new instance")
        return super().__new__(cls)

    def __init__(self):
        print("Initializing the instance")

obj = MyClass()
```

Output:

Creating a new instance

Initializing the instance

- **Explanation**: First, the __new__ method is called to create the object, and then the __init__ method is called to initialize the object's attributes.

7. How Does Python Handle Multiple Inheritance?

Question: *How does Python handle multiple inheritance and the Method Resolution Order (MRO)?*

Answer:
Python handles multiple inheritance through the **Method**

Resolution Order (MRO), which determines the order in which classes are considered when looking for methods. The MRO is based on the **C3 Linearization algorithm**.

Here's an example to understand the MRO:

```python
class A:
    def method(self):
        print("Method in class A")


class B(A):
    def method(self):
        print("Method in class B")


class C(A):
    def method(self):
        print("Method in class C")


class D(B, C):
    pass


d = D()
d.method()  # Output: Method in class B
```

- **Explanation**: In the class D, which inherits from both B and C, the MRO ensures that the method from class B is called first. The method() is executed according to the order defined by Python's MRO.

Mastering decorators, metaclasses, and Python internals will not only give you an edge in interviews but also enable you to write more efficient, reusable, and elegant code. These advanced concepts showcase your deep understanding of Python, making you a standout candidate. By practicing these techniques and understanding their inner workings, you'll be well on your way to acing your Python interview like a pro.

MASTERING SORTING AND SEARCHING ALGORITHMS

Sorting and searching are fundamental algorithms that are often tested in coding interviews, especially for Python developers. Interviewers focus on your understanding of these algorithms to evaluate your problem-solving abilities and to assess how well you optimize code for large datasets. In this chapter, we will cover the most commonly asked sorting and searching problems along with their solutions.

1. Sorting Algorithms

Sorting is the process of arranging elements in a particular order (ascending or descending). Sorting algorithms are essential for efficient data retrieval and organization. Below are the top sorting algorithms commonly asked in Python interviews.

Bubble Sort

Question: Implement the Bubble Sort algorithm.

Answer: Bubble Sort works by repeatedly stepping through the list to be sorted, comparing adjacent elements, and swapping them if they are in the wrong order. The process continues until the list is sorted.

```
def bubble_sort(arr):
    n = len(arr)
    for i in range(n):
        swapped = False
        for j in range(0, n-i-1):
            if arr[j] > arr[j+1]:
                arr[j], arr[j+1] = arr[j+1], arr[j]
                swapped = True
        if not swapped:
            break
    return arr
```

Time Complexity:
- Best Case: O(n)
- Worst Case: O(n^2)
- Space Complexity: O(1)

Key Interview Point:
Bubble Sort is inefficient for large datasets due to its time complexity of O(n^2) in the worst case. Be prepared to explain this limitation in interviews.

Selection Sort

Question: How does Selection Sort work, and implement it in Python.

Answer: Selection Sort divides the list into two parts: the sorted part and the unsorted part. The algorithm repeatedly selects the smallest (or largest) element from the unsorted part and swaps it with the first unsorted element.

```python
def selection_sort(arr):
    for i in range(len(arr)):
        min_index = i
        for j in range(i+1, len(arr)):
            if arr[j] < arr[min_index]:
                min_index = j
        arr[i], arr[min_index] = arr[min_index], arr[i]
    return arr
```

Time Complexity:
- Best, Worst, and Average Case: $O(n^2)$
- Space Complexity: $O(1)$

Key Interview Point:
Although Selection Sort is easy to understand and implement, it has a quadratic time complexity, which makes it inefficient for large datasets.

Quick Sort

Question: Explain the Quick Sort algorithm and implement it in Python.

Answer: Quick Sort is a divide-and-conquer algorithm. It works by selecting a pivot element and partitioning the array into two sub-arrays (elements less than the pivot and elements greater than the pivot). It then recursively sorts the sub-arrays.

```python
def quick_sort(arr):
```

```python
if len(arr) <= 1:
    return arr
pivot = arr[len(arr) // 2]
left = [x for x in arr if x < pivot]
middle = [x for x in arr if x == pivot]
right = [x for x in arr if x > pivot]
return quick_sort(left) + middle + quick_sort(right)
```

Time Complexity:

- Best and Average Case: O(n log n)
- Worst Case: O(n^2)
- Space Complexity: O(log n)

Key Interview Point:

Quick Sort's worst-case time complexity is O(n^2), but it performs well on average. Optimizing the choice of pivot (e.g., using the median of three) can help reduce the likelihood of hitting the worst-case scenario.

Merge Sort

Question: Implement Merge Sort and explain its working.

Answer: Merge Sort is a divide-and-conquer algorithm that splits the array into two halves, recursively sorts them, and merges them back into a sorted array.

```python
def merge_sort(arr):
    if len(arr) <= 1:
        return arr
    mid = len(arr) // 2
```

```python
    left = merge_sort(arr[:mid])
    right = merge_sort(arr[mid:])

    return merge(left, right)

def merge(left, right):
    result = []
    i = j = 0
    while i < len(left) and j < len(right):
        if left[i] < right[j]:
            result.append(left[i])
            i += 1
        else:
            result.append(right[j])
            j += 1
    result.extend(left[i:])
    result.extend(right[j:])
    return result
```

Time Complexity:

- Best, Worst, and Average Case: O(n log n)
- Space Complexity: O(n)

Key Interview Point:
Merge Sort is stable and guarantees O(n log n) performance, but it requires extra space for the temporary sub-arrays.

2. Searching Algorithms

Searching algorithms are critical for finding an element in a data structure. Below are some popular searching algorithms frequently asked in Python interviews.

Linear Search

Question: Implement Linear Search.

Answer: Linear Search works by iterating over all elements in the list and checking if the target element matches any of them. It's simple but inefficient for large datasets.

```python
def linear_search(arr, target):
    for i in range(len(arr)):
        if arr[i] == target:
            return i
    return -1
```

Time Complexity:
- Best Case: O(1)
- Worst Case: O(n)
- Space Complexity: O(1)

Key Interview Point:
Linear Search is often used when the list is unsorted, but for sorted data, more efficient search algorithms like Binary Search should be preferred.

Binary Search

Question: Implement Binary Search for a sorted list.

Answer: Binary Search is an efficient algorithm for finding an element in a sorted list by repeatedly dividing the search interval in half.

```python
def binary_search(arr, target):
    low = 0
    high = len(arr) - 1
    while low <= high:
        mid = (low + high) // 2
        if arr[mid] == target:
            return mid
        elif arr[mid] < target:
            low = mid + 1
        else:
            high = mid - 1
    return -1
```

Time Complexity:
- Best Case: O(1)
- Worst and Average Case: O(log n)
- Space Complexity: O(1)

Key Interview Point:
Binary Search is much faster than Linear Search for large datasets, but it requires the list to be sorted beforehand.

Binary Search Variants

Question: Implement Binary Search for the first or last occurrence of a target element in a sorted array.

Answer: In some cases, you may need to find the first or last occurrence of an element. You can modify Binary Search to return the first or last index.

```python
def first_occurrence(arr, target):
    low, high = 0, len(arr) - 1
    result = -1
    while low <= high:
        mid = (low + high) // 2
        if arr[mid] == target:
            result = mid
            high = mid - 1
        elif arr[mid] < target:
            low = mid + 1
        else:
            high = mid - 1
    return result


def last_occurrence(arr, target):
    low, high = 0, len(arr) - 1
    result = -1
    while low <= high:
        mid = (low + high) // 2
        if arr[mid] == target:
            result = mid
            low = mid + 1
```

```
    elif arr[mid] < target:
        low = mid + 1
    else:
        high = mid - 1
return result
```

Time Complexity:

- Best, Worst, and Average Case: O(log n)
- Space Complexity: O(1)

Sorting and searching algorithms are fundamental to solving a wide range of programming problems. During Python coding interviews, you may encounter both basic and advanced variations of these algorithms. Understanding their core principles, time complexities, and when to use each one will help you stand out as a pro in your interview. Make sure to practice solving problems that require sorting and searching to reinforce your skills.

By mastering algorithms like **Bubble Sort**, **Selection Sort**, **Quick Sort**, **Merge Sort**, **Linear Search**, and **Binary Search**, you can confidently answer these common Python interview questions and impress your interviewers with your problem-solving skills.

CRACKING CODING CHALLENGES: PATTERNS AND STRATEGIES

When it comes to Python interviews, mastering **problem-solving techniques** is as crucial as having knowledge of the language itself. Most coding challenges can be boiled down to familiar patterns, and recognizing these patterns allows you to solve complex problems more efficiently. This chapter covers **two-pointer techniques** and **recursion**, two essential strategies that will help you tackle a wide variety of coding questions.

1. Two-Pointer Technique

The **two-pointer technique** is used to solve problems involving arrays or lists where you need to compare two elements at different positions. It works by having two pointers traverse the list, typically starting from the beginning and end, and moving toward each other. This technique is especially useful in problems related to **sorting**, **subarrays**, **palindromes**, **pairs** of numbers, and **string manipulation**.

Common Use Cases

- **Finding pairs that sum up to a target value.**
- **Checking if a string is a palindrome.**
- **Rearranging arrays or lists.**

- **Finding the maximum or minimum values in a subset of elements.**

Problem 1: Two Sum (Pair with Target Sum)

Problem: Given an array of integers, find two numbers such that they add up to a specific target.

```python
def two_sum(nums, target):
    left, right = 0, len(nums) - 1
    while left < right:
        current_sum = nums[left] + nums[right]
        if current_sum == target:
            return [left, right]
        elif current_sum < target:
            left += 1
        else:
            right -= 1
    return -1
```

Explanation:

- We initialize two pointers, left at the beginning and right at the end of the array.
- We calculate the sum of the two elements at left and right.
- If the sum equals the target, we return their indices.
- If the sum is less than the target, we move the left pointer to the right to increase the sum.
- If the sum is greater than the target, we move the right pointer to the left to decrease the sum.

Problem 2: Palindrome Check

Problem: Check if a string is a palindrome.

```python
def is_palindrome(s):
    left, right = 0, len(s) - 1
    while left < right:
        if s[left] != s[right]:
            return False
        left += 1
        right -= 1
    return True
```

Explanation:

- This solution uses two pointers, left starting at the beginning and right starting at the end of the string.
- We compare the characters at the left and right pointers.
- If they are equal, we move left one step forward and right one step backward.
- If at any point they are not equal, we return False, as the string is not a palindrome.

---

2. Recursion

Recursion is a technique where a function calls itself in order to solve smaller instances of the same problem. In interviews, **recursive solutions** are often used for problems related to **trees, graphs**, and **divide-and-conquer** algorithms. Although recursion is powerful, it's essential to understand the base case and how to break the problem down into smaller sub-problems.

Common Use Cases

- **Tree Traversals** (pre-order, in-order, post-order).
- **Finding the factorial of a number.**
- **Fibonacci sequence.**
- **Solving problems that involve breaking a large problem into smaller sub-problems.**

Problem 1: Factorial of a Number

Problem: Calculate the factorial of a given number n.

```python
def factorial(n):
    if n == 0 or n == 1:
        return 1
    return n * factorial(n - 1)
```

Explanation:

- The base case is $n == 0$ or $n == 1$, where the factorial of both is 1.
- For other values of n, the function calls itself with $n - 1$ and multiplies the result by n.
- This continues until it reaches the base case, at which point the recursion starts to unwind and the final result is computed.

Problem 2: Fibonacci Sequence

Problem: Find the nth Fibonacci number.

```python
def fibonacci(n):
    if n <= 1:
        return n
    return fibonacci(n - 1) + fibonacci(n - 2)
```

Explanation:

- The base case is when n is 0 or 1, where we return n.
- For other values of n, we recursively calculate the sum of the previous two Fibonacci numbers (fibonacci(n - 1) and fibonacci(n - 2)).
- This problem can be optimized with **memoization** to avoid redundant calculations, but the recursive solution showcases the core concept.

Problem 3: Merge Sort (Divide and Conquer)

Problem: Sort an array using the Merge Sort algorithm.

```python
def merge_sort(arr):
    if len(arr) <= 1:
        return arr

    mid = len(arr) // 2
    left_half = merge_sort(arr[:mid])
    right_half = merge_sort(arr[mid:])

    return merge(left_half, right_half)

def merge(left, right):
    sorted_list = []
    while left and right:
        if left[0] < right[0]:
```

```
        sorted_list.append(left.pop(0))
    else:
        sorted_list.append(right.pop(0))


    sorted_list.extend(left or right)
    return sorted_list
```

Explanation:
- **Divide**: The array is divided into two halves recursively until each half has only one element.
- **Conquer**: The merge function combines the two halves into a sorted array.
- **Base case**: If the array has one or zero elements, it is already sorted, so we return the array as is.
- **Efficiency**: Merge Sort is efficient with a time complexity of O(n log n) and works well with large data sets.

3. Combining Two-Pointer Technique with Recursion

Some problems require combining both techniques to solve efficiently. For example, we can use recursion in combination with two pointers to solve problems like searching for pairs, reversing a list, or balancing a tree.

Problem: Reverse a Linked List (Two-pointer with Recursion)

```
def reverse_linked_list(head):
    if not head or not head.next:
        return head
```

```
rest = reverse_linked_list(head.next)

head.next.next = head

head.next = None

return rest
```

Explanation:
- The recursive approach breaks down the problem into smaller sub-problems where each node is reversed.
- The base case is when the node is None or the last node (head.next is None).
- As recursion unfolds, each node points to its previous node, effectively reversing the list.

4. Strategy for Solving Coding Challenges Efficiently

While mastering techniques like two-pointer and recursion is essential, how you approach coding challenges during interviews is equally crucial. Here are some strategies to help you solve problems efficiently:

1. Understand the Problem

- **Clarify requirements**: Ask questions to clarify edge cases, inputs, and outputs.
- **Break down the problem**: Understand what is being asked and identify the constraints.

2. Start with a Naive Solution

- **Brute force**: Begin with a simple brute force solution to understand the problem fully.
- **Identify inefficiencies**: Afterward, optimize the brute force solution.

3. Optimize Your Approach

- **Look for patterns**: Identify common problem-solving patterns such as sliding windows, backtracking, or divide and conquer.
- **Think about time and space complexity**: Ensure your solution is optimal and scalable.

4. Edge Cases and Testing

- **Test edge cases**: Always test with edge cases such as empty arrays, one-element arrays, or large inputs.
- **Iterate and refine**: If the initial solution doesn't work, iterate over the problem to refine it.

Mastering coding challenges requires a combination of **understanding the problem**, **choosing the right approach**, and **optimizing your solution**. The two-pointer technique and recursion are invaluable tools in your coding toolbox, but mastering them requires consistent practice. By using strategies to tackle problems, optimizing your solutions, and improving your problem-solving skills, you can confidently face Python interviews and crack them like a pro.

DYNAMIC PROGRAMMING MADE SIMPLE

Dynamic Programming (DP) is an advanced algorithmic technique used to solve problems that can be broken down into overlapping subproblems. It is often used when the problem involves making decisions that can be built incrementally. Instead of solving the same subproblem multiple times, DP saves the results of each subproblem to avoid redundant work. Here, we focus on answering commonly asked interview questions on dynamic programming that will help you ace your Python interview.

1. What is Dynamic Programming?

Dynamic Programming is a method for solving complex problems by breaking them down into simpler subproblems and storing the results of these subproblems to avoid redundant calculations. Unlike divide and conquer, DP solves overlapping subproblems by caching their results.

Example Problem: Fibonacci Series The Fibonacci sequence can be solved using DP to store previously computed results:

```python
def fibonacci(n):
    dp = [0] * (n + 1)
```

```
dp[1] = 1
for i in range(2, n + 1):
    dp[i] = dp[i - 1] + dp[i - 2]
return dp[n]
```

Here, dp[i] stores the result of fib(i), eliminating the need to recompute it.

2. How do you recognize when to use Dynamic Programming?

Dynamic Programming is applicable when:

- The problem can be divided into smaller, overlapping subproblems.
- There are optimal substructure and overlapping subproblems.
- It can be solved with memoization or tabulation.

Example Problem: 0/1 Knapsack Problem

Given a set of items, each with a weight and value, find the maximum value of items that can be included in a knapsack of capacity W. Using DP:

```
def knapsack(weights, values, W):
    n = len(weights)
    dp = [[0] * (W + 1) for _ in range(n + 1)]

    for i in range(1, n + 1):
        for w in range(W + 1):
            if weights[i - 1] <= w:
```

```
        dp[i][w] = max(dp[i - 1][w], values[i - 1] + dp[i - 1][w -
weights[i - 1]])

    else:

        dp[i][w] = dp[i - 1][w]


    return dp[n][W]
```

In this problem, the DP table stores the results of subproblems to avoid recomputation.

3. What is the difference between Memoization and Tabulation in Dynamic Programming?

Memoization is a top-down approach. In this method, we solve the problem recursively and store the result of each subproblem in a cache (usually a dictionary or array). If the same subproblem is encountered again, we simply return the stored result.

Example: Fibonacci with Memoization

```
def fibonacci_memo(n, memo={}):

    if n in memo:

        return memo[n]

    if n <= 1:

        return n

    memo[n]    =    fibonacci_memo(n    -    1,    memo)    +
fibonacci_memo(n - 2, memo)

    return memo[n]
```

●

Tabulation is a bottom-up approach. We start solving the smallest subproblem and gradually build up to the original problem. We usually use an array or table to store the results of subproblems.

Example: Fibonacci with Tabulation

```
def fibonacci_tab(n):
    dp = [0] * (n + 1)
    dp[1] = 1
    for i in range(2, n + 1):
        dp[i] = dp[i - 1] + dp[i - 2]
    return dp[n]
```

-

4. Can you explain the Time and Space Complexity of Dynamic Programming?

- The **time complexity** of DP problems depends on the number of subproblems and the amount of work done per subproblem. For example, in the Fibonacci series with DP, there are n subproblems and constant time work per subproblem, resulting in a time complexity of **O(n)**.
- The **space complexity** is determined by the space required to store the results of subproblems. For memoization, the space complexity is typically **O(n)** because of the storage for the cache. For tabulation, the space complexity is also **O(n)** for the DP table.

5. What is the Longest Common Subsequence (LCS) Problem?

The LCS problem involves finding the longest sequence that appears in both strings, maintaining their order. It is commonly solved using DP.

Example Problem: Longest Common Subsequence Given two strings s1 and s2, find the length of their longest common subsequence.

```python
def lcs(s1, s2):
    n, m = len(s1), len(s2)
    dp = [[0] * (m + 1) for _ in range(n + 1)]

    for i in range(1, n + 1):
        for j in range(1, m + 1):
            if s1[i - 1] == s2[j - 1]:
                dp[i][j] = 1 + dp[i - 1][j - 1]
            else:
                dp[i][j] = max(dp[i - 1][j], dp[i][j - 1])

    return dp[n][m]
```

6. What is the Coin Change Problem?

The Coin Change problem asks for the minimum number of coins needed to make a given amount using a set of denominations. This is a classic DP problem.

Example Problem: Coin Change Given a list of coins and a total amount, determine the fewest number of coins needed to make the amount.

```python
def coin_change(coins, amount):
    dp = [float('inf')] * (amount + 1)
    dp[0] = 0
```

```
for i in range(1, amount + 1):
    for coin in coins:
        if i - coin >= 0:
            dp[i] = min(dp[i], dp[i - coin] + 1)


return dp[amount] if dp[amount] != float('inf') else -1
```

7. What is the Minimum Path Sum in a Grid?

In this problem, you're given a 2D grid with non-negative integers. You need to find a path from the top-left to the bottom-right corner of the grid, where you can only move right or down, and the sum of the path is minimized.

Example Problem: Minimum Path Sum

```
def min_path_sum(grid):
    m, n = len(grid), len(grid[0])
    dp = [[0] * n for _ in range(m)]


    dp[0][0] = grid[0][0]


    for i in range(1, m):
        dp[i][0] = dp[i - 1][0] + grid[i][0]


    for j in range(1, n):
```

```
    dp[0][j] = dp[0][j - 1] + grid[0][j]


for i in range(1, m):

    for j in range(1, n):

        dp[i][j] = min(dp[i - 1][j], dp[i][j - 1]) + grid[i][j]


return dp[m - 1][n - 1]
```

8. What is the Longest Increasing Subsequence (LIS) Problem?

The LIS problem asks for the length of the longest subsequence that is strictly increasing.

Example Problem: Longest Increasing Subsequence

```
def lis(nums):

    if not nums:

        return 0


    dp = [1] * len(nums)


    for i in range(1, len(nums)):

        for j in range(i):

            if nums[i] > nums[j]:

                dp[i] = max(dp[i], dp[j] + 1)
```

```
return max(dp)
```

9. How do you approach the "Knapsack Problem" with Dynamic Programming?

The 0/1 Knapsack problem asks for the maximum value that can be obtained by filling a knapsack of limited capacity with items having both weight and value. DP is used to store the best results for different capacities.

```
def knapsack(weights, values, W):
    n = len(weights)
    dp = [[0] * (W + 1) for _ in range(n + 1)]

    for i in range(1, n + 1):
        for w in range(W + 1):
            if weights[i - 1] <= w:
                dp[i][w] = max(dp[i - 1][w], values[i - 1] + dp[i - 1][w - weights[i - 1]])
            else:
                dp[i][w] = dp[i - 1][w]

    return dp[n][W]
```

Dynamic Programming can be a challenging concept to grasp

initially, but once you understand its fundamental principles and how to recognize problems that require it, you'll be able to solve a wide range of complex algorithmic problems efficiently. Keep practicing with real-world interview questions like the ones listed above, and soon you'll be answering them like a pro in your Python interviews!

SOLVING REAL-WORLD PROBLEMS WITH PYTHON

In this chapter, we'll explore how Python can be applied to solve real-world problems, which is an essential skill for acing technical interviews. By solving practical problems, you will gain a deeper understanding of how Python's syntax and libraries are used to address everyday challenges in industries like web development, data science, automation, and more.

Problem 1: File Handling and Data Manipulation

Interview Question:
Q: *How would you read and process large data files efficiently using Python?*

Answer:
Python provides powerful libraries like csv, json, and pandas to handle and manipulate large datasets efficiently. Here's a basic solution using Python to process CSV data:

```
import csv
```

```python
def read_large_csv(file_path):

    with open(file_path, mode='r') as file:

        csv_reader = csv.reader(file)

        for row in csv_reader:

            # Process each row

            print(row)


# Example usage

read_large_csv('large_data.csv')
```

In interviews, candidates are expected to explain not just how they would solve the problem, but also consider edge cases such as file size, handling missing data, and optimizing for speed.

For large files, Python's pandas library can be leveraged for more complex operations like filtering or aggregating data:

```python
import pandas as pd


def process_data(file_path):

    df = pd.read_csv(file_path)
```

```
    df_filtered = df[df['age'] > 30]  # Filter data for people older
than 30

    print(df_filtered)


# Example usage

process_data('data.csv')
```

Problem 2: Web Scraping

Interview Question:
Q: *How would you scrape data from a webpage using Python?*

Answer:
Web scraping is a common task, and Python makes it easier with libraries like BeautifulSoup and requests. Here's a simple example that extracts all links from a webpage:

```
import requests

from bs4 import BeautifulSoup


def scrape_links(url):

    response = requests.get(url)

    soup = BeautifulSoup(response.text, 'html.parser')
```

```
links = soup.find_all('a')


for link in links:

    print(link.get('href'))


# Example usage

scrape_links('https://example.com')
```

In an interview, you might be asked to modify this script to extract specific information or handle different types of data such as images or tables. Make sure to also discuss how to manage rate limits, handle potential errors, and ensure compliance with the website's terms of service.

Problem 3: Automating Tasks with Python

Interview Question:
Q: *How would you automate a repetitive task like renaming files in a directory?*

Answer:
Automation is one of Python's strengths, and solving repetitive tasks can be done efficiently with simple scripts. For renaming files in a directory, you can use Python's os library:

```
import os
```

```
def rename_files(directory):

    for filename in os.listdir(directory):

        if filename.endswith('.txt'):

            new_name = filename.replace('old', 'new')

            os.rename(os.path.join(directory,                    filename),
os.path.join(directory, new_name))


# Example usage

rename_files('/path/to/directory')
```

In an interview, interviewers may ask how to handle potential issues like file permissions, checking for existing file names, or processing files recursively in subdirectories.

Problem 4: Data Analysis with Pandas

Interview Question:
Q: *Given a dataset, how would you find the average of a particular column and filter data based on a condition?*

Answer:
For this problem, Python's pandas library is incredibly useful for quick and efficient data manipulation. Here's an example:

```python
import pandas as pd

def analyze_data(file_path):

    df = pd.read_csv(file_path)

    average_salary = df['salary'].mean()  # Calculate the average salary

    print(f"Average Salary: {average_salary}")


    # Filter data for employees in a specific department

    hr_employees = df[df['department'] == 'HR']

    print(hr_employees)


# Example usage

analyze_data('employees.csv')
```

This problem tests your ability to analyze data and use Python for common data analysis tasks, a crucial skill in many technical roles.

Problem 5: Building a Simple API with Flask

Interview Question:

Q: *How would you build a simple web API using Python?*

Answer:
For web development tasks, Python's Flask is a lightweight framework that makes building web APIs quick and simple. Here's how you can create a basic REST API:

```python
from flask import Flask, jsonify


app = Flask(__name__)


@app.route('/api/v1/hello', methods=['GET'])

def hello():

    return jsonify(message="Hello, World!")


if __name__ == '__main__':

    app.run(debug=True)
```

This Flask application will start a local web server and return a "Hello, World!" message when you access http://127.0.0.1:5000/api/v1/hello. In an interview, you should also discuss how to add other HTTP methods (like POST, PUT, DELETE), error handling, and data validation.

Problem 6: Working with Databases

Interview Question:
Q: *How would you interact with a database in Python?*

Answer:
For this, Python provides the sqlite3 library for simple SQLite databases or libraries like SQLAlchemy for more advanced database interaction. Here's an example of how to interact with a SQLite database:

```python
import sqlite3


def create_database():

    conn = sqlite3.connect('example.db')

    cursor = conn.cursor()


    # Create a table

    cursor.execute('''CREATE TABLE IF NOT EXISTS employees

                (id INTEGER PRIMARY KEY, name TEXT, salary
REAL)''')


    # Insert data

    cursor.execute("INSERT INTO employees (name, salary)
VALUES (?, ?)", ('John Doe', 50000))
```

```
conn.commit()


# Query the data

cursor.execute("SELECT * FROM employees")

rows = cursor.fetchall()

for row in rows:

    print(row)


conn.close()


# Example usage

create_database()
```

In an interview, you may be asked to perform operations like querying with joins, handling transactions, or ensuring database integrity with constraints.

Problem 7: Machine Learning Model Deployment

Interview Question:
Q: *How would you deploy a machine learning model in Python?*

Answer:
Deploying a machine learning model involves more than just

building the model; it also includes creating a service that can interact with the model for real-time predictions. Using Flask and pickle (or joblib), you can deploy models quickly. Here's how:

Train and pickle the model (this can be done in a Jupyter notebook or script):

```python
import pickle

from sklearn.ensemble import RandomForestClassifier


# Dummy training

model = RandomForestClassifier()

model.fit(X_train, y_train)


# Save the model to a file

with open('model.pkl', 'wb') as f:

    pickle.dump(model, f)
```

1.

Build a Flask API to serve the model:

```python
from flask import Flask, request, jsonify

import pickle


app = Flask(__name__)
```

```python
# Load the pre-trained model

with open('model.pkl', 'rb') as f:

    model = pickle.load(f)


@app.route('/predict', methods=['POST'])

def predict():

    data = request.get_json() # Get data from the request

    prediction = model.predict([data['features']])

    return jsonify(prediction=prediction.tolist())


if __name__ == '__main__':

    app.run(debug=True)
```

2.

In an interview, ensure you explain how the deployment process works, the use of REST APIs, and the tools you used (like Flask, pickle, or Docker for containerization).

This chapter demonstrated how Python is a powerful tool to solve real-world problems across multiple domains, including data manipulation, web scraping, automation, API creation, and machine learning model deployment. By practicing these problems and understanding their solutions, you'll be well-prepared to face Python-based challenges in technical interviews.

In an interview setting, remember that interviewers are not just looking for the solution—they are assessing your thought process, problem-solving ability, and coding practices. Always explain your approach clearly, handle edge cases, and optimize your code where necessary. Practicing these problems will make you feel confident and prepared for any real-world challenge thrown your way.

MOCK INTERVIEWS AND PRACTICE SESSIONS

When preparing for a Python interview, technical knowledge is essential, but mastering how to present your skills under pressure is just as important. Mock interviews and practice sessions simulate real interview scenarios and are invaluable tools for refining your performance. The purpose of mock interviews is not only to assess your technical abilities but also to build confidence and improve your communication skills. In this chapter, we'll cover how to set up mock interviews, practice effectively, and gain the most from each session.

Step 1: Understand the Importance of Mock Interviews

Mock interviews are designed to mimic the actual interview experience. They help you:

- **Identify Weak Areas**: Mock interviews reveal areas where your knowledge is lacking, allowing you to focus on improving them.
- **Simulate Pressure**: Interviews often come with time constraints and pressure to perform well. Mock interviews replicate this experience, so you can get comfortable with high-stress situations.

- **Improve Communication**: Answering questions clearly and concisely is critical. Mock interviews allow you to refine your explanation skills.
- **Boost Confidence**: Regular mock interviews help reduce anxiety, so when the real interview comes, you'll feel ready to tackle any question confidently.

Step 2: Set Up the Mock Interview Environment

Creating the right environment for your mock interview is crucial to simulate a real interview experience. Follow these guidelines:

1. **Choose a Quiet Space**: Conduct the mock interview in a quiet place where you can focus without distractions.
2. **Dress the Part**: Dressing professionally for the mock interview helps create a formal environment and primes your mind for the actual interview.
3. **Time Your Sessions**: Stick to a strict schedule during your mock interview to get used to the time constraints often present in real interviews. For coding problems, set a timer to complete tasks within 20-30 minutes.
4. **Use Video Calls for Remote Interviews**: If your real interview is remote, use video calling platforms (e.g., Zoom, Google Meet) for your mock interview to practice virtual communication skills.

Step 3: Choose the Right Mock Interview Format

Mock interviews can be structured in several ways, depending on your needs:

1. **Solo Practice**: For some candidates, solving coding problems and explaining solutions aloud to yourself can be effective. Record your answers and review them to evaluate

your performance.

2. **Peer-to-Peer**: Practice with a friend or peer who can play the role of the interviewer. They can ask you common Python interview questions and provide feedback afterward.

3. **Professional Mock Interviews**: Platforms like *Pramp*, *Interviewing.io*, and *Gainlo* offer mock interviews with experienced professionals. These services are highly valuable as they give you the chance to practice with individuals who are familiar with the latest interview trends.

Step 4: Prepare a List of Common Python Interview Questions

To make the most of your mock interview sessions, practice answering the questions that frequently appear in Python interviews. Here are some of the most commonly asked questions:

1. Reverse a String in Python

Question: Write a Python program to reverse a string without using any in-built functions.

Answer:

```python
def reverse_string(s):

    return s[::-1]


# Test case

print(reverse_string("Python"))  # Output: nohtyP
```

2. Find the Maximum Occurring Character in a String

Question: Given a string, find the most frequent character in it.

Answer:

```python
from collections import Counter

def max_occurring_char(s):
    count = Counter(s)
    return count.most_common(1)[0][0]

# Test case
print(max_occurring_char("Programming"))  # Output: r
```

3. Check if a Number is Prime

Question: Write a function to check if a number is prime or not.

Answer:

```python
def is_prime(n):
```

```
    if n <= 1:

        return False

    for i in range(2, int(n**0.5) + 1):

        if n % i == 0:

            return False

    return True


# Test case

print(is_prime(11))  # Output: True
```

4. Find the Fibonacci Sequence

Question: Write a program to print the Fibonacci sequence up to n terms.

Answer:

```
def fibonacci(n):

    a, b = 0, 1

    for _ in range(n):

        print(a, end=" ")

        a, b = b, a + b
```

```
# Test case

fibonacci(5)  # Output: 0 1 1 2 3
```

5. Remove Duplicates from a List

Question: Write a Python function that removes duplicate values from a list.

Answer:

```
def remove_duplicates(lst):

    return list(set(lst))
```

```
# Test case

print(remove_duplicates([1, 2, 2, 3, 4, 4]))  # Output: [1, 2, 3, 4]
```

Step 5: Answering Like a Pro

When answering questions during your mock interview, follow these best practices:

1. **Clarify the Problem**: If you don't understand the question, ask clarifying questions. This shows the interviewer that you are thinking critically before diving into a solution.

Example: "Could you clarify whether I should assume the input will always be a valid string, or should I handle edge cases like empty strings?"

2. **Explain Your Approach**: Before jumping into coding, explain your thought process. This allows the interviewer to follow your reasoning, and they can offer suggestions if you're on the wrong track.
   Example: "I will first check if the string is empty, then iterate through the string to count the characters and find the maximum occurring one."

3. **Write Clean Code**: Even during mock interviews, focus on writing clean, readable code. Use meaningful variable names and comment where necessary. Good coding habits reflect well on you.

4. **Optimize Your Solution**: Whenever possible, explain the time complexity and space complexity of your solution. If the interviewer suggests an optimization, be open to adapting your approach.
   Example: "This solution has a time complexity of $O(n)$ due to the single iteration through the string."

5. **Test Your Code**: Always run test cases to check if your solution works correctly. If you notice an issue, debug your code out loud, explaining what you would check first.

Step 6: Post-Interview Reflection and Feedback

After completing your mock interview, take time to reflect on your performance:

1. **Evaluate Your Answers**: Did you answer the question confidently? Did you explain your thought process clearly? Did you follow up with an optimal solution?

2. **Ask for Feedback**: Request feedback from your mock interviewer (whether it's a peer or a professional). Feedback will help you understand where you can improve.

3. **Identify Areas of Improvement**: If you struggled with certain types of questions (e.g., algorithms, data structures, or system design), note them down and focus on those areas during your next practice session.
4. **Practice Regularly**: The key to success is consistency. Schedule regular mock interview sessions to continuously refine your skills. As you approach the real interview, make sure to simulate full-length mock interviews to replicate the complete experience.

Step 7: Using Mock Interviews for Behavioral Practice

While technical interviews are critical, many companies also evaluate behavioral aspects in interviews. Use mock interviews as an opportunity to practice both technical and behavioral questions.

- **Prepare for HR Questions**: Expect questions like "Tell me about yourself," "Why do you want to work here?" and "Where do you see yourself in five years?" Practice answering them with a focus on how your skills align with the company's values and goals.
- **Simulate Stressful Scenarios**: In mock interviews, it's also important to simulate high-pressure situations where you might be interrupted or asked to solve problems on the spot. This helps you stay calm and focused under stress.

Mock interviews are one of the most effective ways to prepare for Python interviews. By simulating real interview conditions, you can identify your strengths and weaknesses, improve your communication skills, and build the confidence needed to perform well. Regular practice, along with constructive feedback, will help you refine your technical and behavioral responses and ultimately boost your chances of landing your desired job.

Stay consistent, be open to feedback, and always strive for improvement. With the right approach and dedication, you'll be ready to answer like a pro and get hired in just 30 days!

BEHAVIORAL ROUNDS: PRESENTING YOUR BEST SELF

In the journey to crack Python interviews, the **technical rounds** often steal the spotlight. However, there's another crucial aspect of the interview process that is just as important—**behavioral rounds**. These rounds focus on understanding who you are as a person, how well you fit into the company culture, and whether your mindset aligns with the organization's values. While technical knowledge is critical, **how you present yourself**, **how you handle stress**, and **how you communicate** can make or break your chances.

In this chapter, we will focus on **preparing for the behavioral interview questions** and mastering the art of presenting yourself as the ideal candidate. These questions typically revolve around your past experiences, your problem-solving approach, how you handle challenges, and how you work with teams. You will find **the most commonly asked HR and behavioral interview questions** along with tips and strategies for answering them like a pro.

1. Tell Me About Yourself.

This is one of the most common opening questions in interviews. Many candidates falter here because they give a long and irrelevant history of their career. This is your chance to summarize who you are, highlighting your technical skills while emphasizing your passion for Python and software development.

Pro Tip: Start by briefly describing your background and professional experience. Follow it up with your achievements and skills relevant to the role. Finally, mention why you are excited about this particular job. Keep it concise and focus on your unique value proposition.

Answer Example:
"I'm a software developer with 3 years of experience, primarily working with Python in developing scalable web applications. I've developed and maintained numerous systems using Django and Flask frameworks and have a strong understanding of data structures and algorithms. My passion for clean code and problem-solving drives me to continuously improve my technical skills. I'm excited about this role because it aligns perfectly with my interest in building high-performance applications and working with a talented team."

2. Why Should We Hire You?

This is an opportunity to make a strong case for why you're the perfect fit for the job. The interviewer is looking for a candidate who can solve the company's problems and contribute to its success.

Pro Tip: Tailor your response to match the company's needs, which you should have researched beforehand. Focus on your Python skills, problem-solving abilities, and how you've successfully handled similar challenges in the past.

Answer Example:
"I believe I am the right fit for this position because I have a strong foundation in Python development, particularly in building scalable applications using Django and Flask. Additionally, I'm highly motivated to solve problems, and

I thrive in collaborative environments. My experience in developing real-time applications and integrating APIs will allow me to contribute immediately to your team's goals. Moreover, my passion for continuous learning ensures I stay up-to-date with the latest technologies and best practices."

3. Tell Me About a Time You Faced a Challenge at Work.

This question tests your problem-solving skills and resilience. Interviewers want to understand how you handle adversity, learn from your experiences, and continue to perform under pressure.

Pro Tip: Use the **STAR Method** (Situation, Task, Action, Result) to structure your answer. This method helps you present a clear, concise response, showing your logical approach to overcoming obstacles.

Answer Example:
Situation: "In my previous role, I was working on a project that required integrating a third-party API to fetch live data. However, the API had frequent downtimes, which impacted our application's reliability."
Task: "My task was to find a solution to ensure the application would work even when the API was down."
Action: "I implemented a fallback mechanism using cached data and set up automated alerts to monitor the API's status. I also optimized the retry logic to handle intermittent failures."
Result: "As a result, we were able to maintain the application's uptime and ensure a seamless user experience, even during API outages."

4. How Do You Handle Deadlines and Multiple Priorities?

Employers want to see if you can manage your time effectively and balance competing demands. This is crucial in the fast-paced tech industry where priorities change quickly.

Pro Tip: Discuss how you prioritize tasks, stay organized, and manage time to meet deadlines.

Answer Example:
"I approach deadlines by breaking down tasks into smaller, manageable chunks and setting clear milestones. When handling multiple priorities, I always focus on delivering high-value tasks first. I regularly communicate with my team to align on priorities and ensure that nothing is missed. I also use task management tools like Jira to stay organized and track my progress."

5. How Do You Deal With Difficult Colleagues or Team Conflicts?

Teamwork is essential in most development roles, and the ability to resolve conflicts and collaborate is highly valued. This question assesses your interpersonal and conflict resolution skills.

Pro Tip: Show your ability to remain calm and professional, and emphasize your willingness to work toward a solution.

Answer Example:
"In situations of conflict, I believe in open communication and addressing issues early on. I try to understand the other person's perspective and find common ground. For example, in one project, a colleague and I had differing opinions on the technical approach to take. I initiated a discussion, where we both shared our views, and we were able to find a middle ground that met the project's objectives. I believe maintaining respect and staying focused on the team's goals is key to resolving conflicts."

6. What is Your Greatest Strength?

This is a classic question designed to assess your self-awareness and confidence. You want to highlight a strength that aligns with the job requirements, especially in terms of technical skills and teamwork.

Pro Tip: Be specific about your strength and provide an example to demonstrate it.

Answer Example:

"My greatest strength is my problem-solving ability. I love tackling complex coding challenges and finding efficient solutions. For instance, I once optimized a slow-running Python application by refactoring its algorithms, which improved performance by 50%. My passion for optimizing code drives me to constantly look for ways to make processes more efficient."

7. What is Your Weakness?

This question helps the interviewer understand your areas of improvement. It's important to be honest but also to show that you are working on your weakness.

Pro Tip: Avoid mentioning a critical weakness that might hinder your ability to perform the job. Instead, talk about a weakness that is not directly related to the role and explain how you're working to improve it.

Answer Example:

"One area I've been working on is improving my ability to delegate tasks effectively. In the past, I've often taken on too much work myself to ensure the quality of the results. However, I've realized that delegation is key to effective teamwork, and I've been practicing this by collaborating more with my colleagues and trusting them with tasks. It has helped me be more productive and empowered my team."

8. Why Do You Want to Work for This Company?

This question assesses whether you've done your research on the company and whether you align with its values and goals. Your answer should show that you're enthusiastic and genuinely interested in the company.

Pro Tip: Mention specific aspects of the company—such as its products, culture, or mission—that resonate with you.

Answer Example:

"I've been following your company for some time and I admire how you're using Python to innovate in the field of machine learning and artificial intelligence. I'm particularly excited about your recent project on XYZ, and I would love to contribute my Python skills and passion for technology to help the team achieve its goals. I'm also impressed by your company's focus on continuous learning and professional development, which aligns with my personal values."

9. Where Do You See Yourself in 5 Years?

This question helps interviewers gauge your long-term career goals and whether they align with the company's growth.

Pro Tip: Focus on how you plan to grow professionally and contribute to the company's success.

Answer Example:
"In five years, I see myself as a senior developer, taking on more leadership responsibilities and mentoring junior team members. I hope to have contributed significantly to several successful projects and helped the company adopt new technologies that improve performance. I'm excited about growing within a company that values innovation and continuous improvement."

10. Do You Have Any Questions for Us?

Always have questions prepared. This is your chance to show your interest in the company and clarify anything you're unsure about.

Pro Tip: Ask thoughtful questions about the team structure, company culture, or the challenges the company is currently facing.

Answer Example:
"Can you tell me more about the current projects the team is working on and the role I would play in them? Also, I'm curious about the professional development opportunities the company offers."

Behavioral rounds are your chance to show the interviewer that you are not only a technically skilled Python developer but also someone who fits the company culture and can handle the demands of the job. By preparing well and practicing your responses, you can confidently present your best self and make a lasting impression.

COMMON PYTHON INTERVIEW QUESTIONS EXPLAINED

Interviews can be daunting, especially when you face challenging Python-related questions. However, with the right preparation and understanding, you can answer these questions confidently and impress your interviewer. In this chapter, we will cover the most frequently asked Python interview questions and provide detailed solutions that will help you ace your next interview.

1. What are Python's key features?

This is one of the most basic questions that you might encounter in a Python interview. The interviewer wants to know whether you understand Python's core advantages.

Answer:

- **Easy Syntax**: Python is designed to be easy to read and write. Its syntax is straightforward, which allows developers to focus more on problem-solving rather than language complexity.
- **Dynamically Typed**: Python does not require explicit declarations for variable types. The type of a variable is determined at runtime, which makes it more flexible but

potentially prone to runtime errors.

- **Interpreted Language**: Python code is executed line by line, which makes debugging easier.
- **Object-Oriented**: Python supports OOP principles such as inheritance, polymorphism, encapsulation, and abstraction, making it versatile for building complex systems.
- **Large Standard Library**: Python has a rich standard library that supports a wide variety of applications, including web development, scientific computing, data analysis, and more.
- **Cross-Platform**: Python can run on different platforms such as Windows, macOS, and Linux, making it highly portable.

2. What is the difference between deepcopy and shallow copy in Python?

This is a commonly asked question when interviewing for roles involving data manipulation and memory management.

Answer:

- **Shallow Copy**: A shallow copy creates a new object but does not recursively copy objects inside the original object. It only copies references to the objects inside. If the original object contains nested objects (like lists inside lists), changes to those nested objects in the shallow copy will also affect the original object.
  - Example: copy.copy()
- **Deep Copy**: A deep copy creates a new object and also recursively copies all the objects inside the original object. As a result, changes made to any object in the deep copy do not affect the original object.
  - Example: copy.deepcopy()

Code Example:

```
import copy
original = [[1, 2], [3, 4]]
shallow = copy.copy(original)
deep = copy.deepcopy(original)

shallow[0][0] = 99
print(original) # [[99, 2], [3, 4]] - shallow copy affects the original
print(deep)    # [[1, 2], [3, 4]] - deep copy remains unaffected
```

---

3. Explain Python's self keyword.

The self keyword is frequently asked in object-oriented programming questions.

Answer:

- self is a reference to the current instance of the class. It is used to access variables and methods that belong to the class.
- In Python, methods in a class always take self as the first parameter, but it is not passed explicitly when calling the method. It is passed implicitly when you call a method from an object.

Code Example:

```
class MyClass:
    def __init__(self, name):
        self.name = name
```

```
def greet(self):
    print(f"Hello, {self.name}")


obj = MyClass("Alice")
obj.greet()  # Output: Hello, Alice
```

---

4. What are Python decorators and how do they work?

Python decorators are widely used in Python and frequently asked in advanced interviews.

Answer:

- A decorator is a function that takes another function (or method) as an argument and adds functionality to it.
- It allows modification of the behavior of a function without changing its source code.
- Decorators are used in various Python libraries (like Flask or Django) for things like logging, authentication, or memoization.

Code Example:

```
def decorator(func):
    def wrapper():
        print("Before function execution")
        func()
        print("After function execution")
    return wrapper
```

```
@decorator
def greet():
    print("Hello!")

greet()
# Output:
# Before function execution
# Hello!
# After function execution
```

---

5. What is the difference between `==` and `is` in Python?

Understanding Python's comparison operators is crucial for avoiding common pitfalls during interviews.

Answer:

- `==` checks if the values of two objects are equal.
- `is` checks if two references point to the same object in memory (i.e., it checks for object identity).

Code Example:

```
a = [1, 2, 3]
b = [1, 2, 3]
c = a

print(a == b)  # True, because their values are the same
```

```
print(a is b)  # False, because they are two different objects in
memory

print(a is c)  # True, because both refer to the same object
```

6. What are Python's built-in data types?

This question tests your understanding of Python's basic building blocks.

Answer: Python has several built-in data types:

- **Numeric Types**: int, float, complex
- **Sequence Types**: list, tuple, range
- **Text Type**: str
- **Mapping Type**: dict
- **Set Types**: set, frozenset
- **Boolean Type**: bool
- **Binary Types**: bytes, bytearray, memoryview
- **None Type**: NoneType

7. How does Python handle memory management?

Memory management is an important aspect of Python, and interviewers often ask this to gauge your knowledge of optimization.

Answer:

- Python uses **automatic memory management**, which includes:
  - **Garbage Collection**: Python uses a reference counting mechanism to track the number of references to an object. When the reference count drops to zero, the object is eligible for garbage collection. Additionally, Python has a cyclic garbage collector that cleans up reference cycles (where objects reference each other).
  - **Memory Pools**: Python uses an internal memory

management system that groups small objects into blocks for efficiency.

- ○ **Memory Allocation**: Python allocates memory for objects dynamically and releases memory when it is no longer in use.

8. What are Python's lambda functions?

Lambda functions are a key concept in functional programming.

Answer:

- A lambda function is an anonymous, inline function defined using the lambda keyword. It is used for creating small, one-line functions without needing to define a full function using def.
- Lambda functions can take any number of arguments, but can only have one expression.

Code Example:

```
add = lambda x, y: x + y

print(add(2, 3)) # Output: 5
```

9. What is the difference between range and xrange in Python?

This is an interview question aimed at distinguishing Python 2.x and Python 3.x behavior.

Answer:

- **Python 2.x**: range() creates a list, whereas xrange() returns an iterator that generates values on demand (lazy evaluation).
- **Python 3.x**: range() behaves like xrange() from Python 2.x; it returns an iterator, and xrange() no longer exists.

10. What is list comprehension in Python?

List comprehension is a concise way to create lists and is a popular topic in Python interviews.

Answer:

- List comprehension provides a syntactically elegant way to generate lists from existing iterables in a single line.
- It reduces the need for loops and makes code more readable.

Code Example:

```
squares = [x**2 for x in range(5)]
print(squares) # Output: [0, 1, 4, 9, 16]
```

This chapter covered some of the most commonly asked Python interview questions along with detailed answers. By practicing these questions and understanding the reasoning behind each answer, you'll be well on your way to acing your next Python interview. Be sure to review the other sections of the book to enhance your problem-solving skills and boost your confidence in technical interviews.

BEYOND THE CODE: LANDING YOUR DREAM JOB

Successfully acing a Python interview involves more than just solving coding challenges; it's about creating a lasting impression, showcasing your skills, and effectively negotiating the job offer. In this chapter, we focus on the practical steps required after the technical interview: resume building, interview follow-ups, and offer negotiation. By following these strategies, you can set yourself apart from other candidates and secure the job of your dreams.

1. Crafting the Perfect Resume for Python Roles

A resume is the first thing that potential employers see, so it's essential to make it stand out. The key to a winning Python resume is showcasing both your technical skills and your problem-solving abilities. Here's how you can structure your Python-specific resume to catch the attention of recruiters:

a) Highlight Relevant Skills Focus on skills directly related to Python development. Make sure to include:

- **Core Python**: Knowledge of data structures, algorithms, object-oriented programming, etc.
- **Python Libraries**: List popular libraries you are proficient in, such as pandas, NumPy, Flask, Django, TensorFlow, or Matplotlib.

- **Frameworks and Tools**: Highlight experience with frameworks like Django, Flask, or FastAPI, and mention familiarity with version control tools (Git), and testing tools (e.g., pytest).
- **Database Knowledge**: Knowledge of databases such as SQL, MySQL, PostgreSQL, or NoSQL databases like MongoDB should also be featured.
- **Version Control and CI/CD Tools**: If you have experience with Git, GitHub, Docker, Jenkins, or similar tools, ensure these are clearly listed.

b) Focus on Projects and Achievements Rather than just listing your job duties, focus on specific projects where Python played a crucial role:

- **Personal Projects**: If you've worked on any Python projects independently, include them. Open-source contributions or coding challenges can also be highlighted.
- **Quantifiable Achievements**: When describing your work in previous roles, use numbers to quantify your impact. For example, "Optimized data processing using Python, reducing execution time by 30%" or "Built an automation script that saved the team 10 hours per week."
- **Project Relevance**: Ensure that the projects listed are relevant to the job you're applying for. If applying for a data scientist role, highlight projects involving data analysis, machine learning, or artificial intelligence.

c) Tailor Your Resume for Each Job Make small adjustments to your resume for each job application. Use keywords from the job description and emphasize your relevant experience. Employers often use Applicant Tracking Systems (ATS) to filter resumes, and optimizing your resume with the correct keywords can increase your chances of passing the ATS filter.

2. Following Up After the Interview

Follow-up emails are a powerful way to reinforce your interest in the role and demonstrate your professionalism. After the interview, sending a well-crafted follow-up email can set you apart from other candidates. Here's how you can write an effective post-interview email:

a) Timing Is Crucial Send your follow-up email within 24 hours of the interview. This shows your enthusiasm and keeps you fresh in the interviewer's mind.

b) Be Grateful and Professional Begin your email by thanking the interviewer for their time and the opportunity. Express appreciation for the conversation and highlight a key part of the interview that you enjoyed or found insightful.

c) Reiterate Your Interest and Fit Reaffirm your interest in the role and how your skills make you a great fit. For example, you can mention a specific problem discussed during the interview and elaborate on how you can help solve it using Python.

d) Be Concise Your follow-up email doesn't need to be long. Keep it short and to the point, with a clear expression of gratitude and a reiteration of why you're excited about the position.

Example Follow-Up Email:

Subject: Thank You for the Interview Opportunity

Dear [Interviewer's Name],

I would like to sincerely thank you for taking the time to interview me for the Python Developer position at [Company Name] yesterday. I really enjoyed our conversation, particularly discussing how Python can be used to optimize data workflows. I believe that my experience with libraries like pandas and NumPy would allow me to contribute meaningfully to the team.

I'm very excited about the opportunity to work at [Company Name] and look forward to hearing back regarding the next steps. Please don't hesitate to reach out if you need any further information.

Best regards,
[Your Name]

3. Negotiating Your Job Offer

Once you've impressed the interviewers and received the job offer, the next critical step is negotiating the terms. Many candidates overlook the power of negotiation, but with the right approach, you can maximize your salary, benefits, and overall job satisfaction.

a) Do Your Research Before entering into negotiations, it's important to research salary ranges for Python developers in your area, taking into account factors like experience, company size, and industry. Websites like Glassdoor, PayScale, and LinkedIn Salary Insights can provide helpful data on average salaries for Python developers.

b) Consider the Entire Compensation Package Salary isn't the only aspect of your offer. Take a holistic approach to your negotiation:

- **Health Benefits**: Health insurance, dental, and vision coverage are important aspects of a compensation package.
- **Stock Options**: If applicable, stock options can significantly increase the overall value of your offer, especially in tech companies.
- **Paid Time Off (PTO)**: Consider how much paid leave (vacation and sick days) you'll receive and if it meets your needs.
- **Work-Life Balance**: Inquire about flexible work hours, remote working opportunities, or any other arrangements that contribute to work-life balance.

c) Be Confident and Professional When negotiating, be confident but also respectful. Express your enthusiasm for the job and your desire to make a fair agreement. For instance:

Example Negotiation Script:

"I'm really excited about this role and believe I can bring a lot of value to the team, particularly with my experience in Python and automation. I was hoping to discuss the base salary as it is slightly below the industry average for my experience level in this region. Based on my research and the skills I would bring to the table, would it be possible to adjust the salary to [desired amount]?"

d) Don't Be Afraid to Walk Away If the offer doesn't meet your expectations and there's no room for flexibility, don't be afraid to politely decline. However, make sure that you leave on good terms. You never know when a better offer or opportunity may come your way.

---

4. Tips for a Successful Job Search

In addition to perfecting your resume and mastering the interview process, here are some additional tips to increase your chances of landing a Python job:

a) Network Actively Leverage LinkedIn to connect with professionals in the Python community, including developers, hiring managers, and recruiters. Attend tech meetups and conferences to expand your network.

b) Contribute to Open Source Projects Contributing to open-source projects can showcase your Python skills and build your credibility in the community. GitHub is an excellent platform to showcase your work.

c) Stay Updated with the Latest Trends Python and its ecosystem are constantly evolving. Stay up to date with new libraries, frameworks, and best practices by following industry blogs, attending webinars, and reading books. Continuous learning will make you a more valuable candidate in the long run.

d) Prepare for Remote Jobs With the growing trend of remote work, be sure to prepare for remote job interviews. Make sure your home office setup is professional, your communication skills are sharp, and you are comfortable using collaboration tools like Zoom, Slack, and GitHub.

Landing your dream Python developer job is not just about having strong technical skills; it's about presenting yourself as a well-rounded professional. By crafting a stellar resume, following up professionally after the interview, and negotiating your offer effectively, you set yourself up for success. Keep refining your skills, learning new Python concepts, and maintaining a proactive approach to your job search, and soon you'll land the job you've been preparing for.